FROM NAGS TO NUMBNUTS

A SKINT DADDY'S GUIDE TO HORSES, HORSE PEOPLE & HORSE SPORTS

DANIEL SKINNER

Illustrated by
LYNN ADAMS

Edited by
SIMON CLARK

OBVIOUS BOOKS

COPYRIGHT

Printed and bound in Great Britain by Clays Ltd, Elcograf S.p.A.

Published by Obvious Books, Bury St Edmunds

www.obviousbooks.co.uk

First Printing 2018.

ISBN 978-1-9164317-0-6

Illustrated by Lynn Adams

www.facebook.com/LynnAdamsIllustration

Read Skint Dressage Daddy online

www.skintdressagedaddy.com

www.facebook.com/skintdressagedaddy

THANKS

I'd like to thank Lynn Adams for providing the wonderful illustrations throughout this book. And my old friend Simon Clark for giving so much time to edit and bash it all into shape. Also, Victoria Brant for offering help and advice.

I'd also like to thank all of the loyal followers who haven't seemed to mind me take the piss out of them for so long. I hope you enjoy it even more in book form.

And of course, I have to thank the two women in my life — CC1 and CC2, without whom I'd have nothing to moan about but love dearly.

CONTENTS

INTRODUCTION

Hello horse people. Welcome to *From Nags to Numbnuts*, which I think you'll find is an indispensable guide to the world of horses, horse sports and all that horse stuff in general.

Over the next hundred or so pages I eventually manage to pad this out to, you'll learn everything from what horses wear to how much it costs to run one. Though I can answer that bit right now: it's fucking loads.

Firstly though, I feel it's only fair to give you a bit more detail about my own experiences with nags and perhaps relate some personal anecdotes about interesting and amusing moments I've shared with our equine friends.

Well, sorry to disappoint but I've got fuck all of those. My experience of horses is purely a financial one; I provide the finances and my daughter has the experiences. The only connection I've had with horses is that I went on a merry-go-round as a small child and threw up. I've also seen City Slickers.

And so, how do I find myself having to wade through a

sea of jodhpurs, show jackets and multi-coloured horse clothing just to get out of my own house to go to work to pay for all the shit I have to wade through in order to go to work?

Well, many, many years ago there was a young man who lived a happy life in a big city, surrounded by his friends. He kept himself busy with the serious business of work and with the even more serious business of enjoying himself.

But then he met a girl, fell in love and settled down. Unfortunately that didn't work out, so he found another one. Frankly that went even more badly than the first, but eventually he found someone that was sort of OK and they stayed together.

Several years passed and they were living in the countryside with two children and too many pets. That would be bad enough, but worse still, for a while they lived next to a small livery yard and the daughter was raised in the presence of horses.

Like a child exposed to drugs and crime while growing up, this had a devastating effect on her and she became hopelessly, woefully addicted. Had she been a better mother, the woman would've shielded her daughter more effectively when the signs started to manifest themselves, or at least tried to drive a stake between her daughter and the love of her life before it became too serious. But no.

Helping muck out at the stable led to occasional lessons; occasional lessons led to weekly lessons; pony club made way for a bit of showjumping and this in turn led to the discovery of dressage and a full-blown love affair began.

Fast forward a few years and the mother and girl have

conspired together to make the poor young man into an older one, and more rapidly than he thinks is natural. His brown hair is turning grey, his language is turning blue and his bank balance is turning red.

That man is me, by the way. It's supposed to be like one of those flashback bits in a movie when the screen goes all wobbly, but just in case it didn't work without any pictures I thought I'd better say.

Which means of course, that the woman is my wife. Love of my life, source of my happiness, drainer of my bank account. And like all romantic, loving couples should, we have affectionate nicknames for each other. I call her Cost Centre One.

Our daughter, now 11, has morphed rapidly from a little girl who used to insist on wearing a tutu while sat on the floor watching Peppa Pig, to someone who's deeply unhappy unless she smells slightly of horse piss. She now dreams only of riding at the Olympics, beating Charlotte Dujardin's score of 93.85761% and owning the world's largest collection of *matchy matchy* shit. And of course, she requires driving back and forth from stables, lessons, and competitions. All of which need paying for. She is known, naturally, as Cost Centre Two.

I think you can see that I'm now somewhat of an expert on all things horse and am fully qualified to provide insightful commentary on this strange and wonderful world. I've spent literally 4, maybe even 5 hours watching the lower echelons of school-age dressage, sometimes with my eyes actually still open, and countless hours listening to CCs 1 and 2 bang on incessantly about bridles and numbnuts and all that other horsey shit they discuss daily over the dinner table — the 'canter banter'.

So, if you're new to nags and all that stuff and are looking to find out more, or maybe an experienced horse person wanting to top up your knowledge and get a better overall picture of the whole thing, then you've come to the right place.

Enjoy.

CHAPTER 1

Are horses addictive?

ARE HORSES ADDICTIVE?

Although I have no particular interest in horses personally, I do see the positives when it comes to a hobby for our child. First and foremost, it takes up a lot of her time, and I've been guaranteed by CC1 that she therefore won't have the opportunity to meet boys for the next several years. I don't own a shotgun, and this will hopefully put off my need to buy one. CC2's happiness is of course my primary concern in life and I dearly hope that she meets a lovely young man and gets married someday. But she has to be at least 25 before she starts looking.

Secondly, it's a healthy outdoor pursuit, and she gets plenty of fresh air and exercise. It's a far healthier hobby than, say, being locked away in a dark bedroom playing computer games. And thirdly, there's all the other shit: you know, being disciplined, having goals, being focussed, meeting challenges, blah blah blah. All the stuff you might see on a motivational poster underneath a photo of a whale.

So, on the face of it, it seems like a pretty good thing

for a kid to get involved in. But hold your horses! It's not that simple! Apart from the desperate, crippling, bank-draining expense of the whole thing, there's also a darker side that I feel we need to discuss at this point. That of addiction.

According to experts, one in three people are addicted to something. It can be almost anything, though the best ones are drugs, alcohol and nicotine. These are of course chemically addictive and so are not just habit-forming but can cause very real physical symptoms when an addict is deprived of them, and that makes the addiction so much harder to break.

If you think this has nothing whatsoever to do with horses, then you clearly haven't met my daughter.

It all starts off so innocently. Usually, an interest in nags is expressed by the child and perhaps there's a request to have an introductory riding lesson. What can possibly go wrong? Well, that sports car you promised yourself in ten years' time, that's what. A single lesson might become a more regular event, and before you know it, your child is actively involved in learning how to ride.

This is where the occasional splashing of cash starts to become more of a constant trickle. If, as a parent, you manage to call it a day at this point, then that trickle can be dammed up nice and early. And if that's where you are now, you should think very carefully about doing just that, because it only takes a long season of heavy horse rainfall and that little money stream can burst its banks and become a raging torrent of foaming banknotes, all originating from the raincloud of your bank account.

Not everyone becomes addicted at this stage though, either as kids or adults. It's a bit like smoking; everyone knows it's highly addictive and very bad for you, but some people try a couple to 'experiment' and never get past the fact that you're just sucking in deadly smoke and making your entire self, clothes and house stink. Others start out quite liking it, but it doesn't really take hold. The financial burden might put them off, or the health implications, or a newfound girlfriend or boyfriend who hates it.

And so it is with the nags, there's no guarantee that exposure at an early age will definitely lead to a full-on dependency. But all I can say is, you're dicing with death. Once the habit forms and manifests itself as regular lessons, then you're on thin fucking ice, my friend.

From lessons, various dreadful things can happen. A popular next step is a 'pony day', whereby you get to spend a few hours stroking small horses and nuzzling your face into their necks, while repeatedly whispering "Oh my god, I love you so much!" at the poor, long-suffering nags. The classic birthday treat for a young and aspiring horse person and all her friends.

From here you might move on to a 'pony camp', which can extend to a few days, or even a week, often camping overnight at a horse hotel. The reason these exist is essentially a deal entered into by two parties — parents and hotel owners — whereby each thinks they're getting something they want. The parents get to offload their offspring for a few, precious days over the school holidays in order to try and claw back some sanity while being allowed to start drinking from lunchtime. And the hotel owner gets some free child labour to help clear up all the horse shit. It's win/win.

Or so they think.

The hotel owners quickly realise that *useful labour* and *a bunch of screaming, gabbling children* aren't the same thing at all, and while the parents might well be initially happy with the financial outlay to get a few days' peace and quiet, there's a very high risk that this will backfire spectacularly over the coming years, maybe even decades, with an overall financial bill running into many, many thousands.

Trust me. I know this from first-hand experience. I recall those innocent pony days and camps of only a few years ago, where CC2 and her gaggle of friends would encircle some poor, hapless nag before stroking and brushing it almost to death. It's a miracle those ponies have any hair left on them by the end of the summer. Surely nothing can survive that amount of love?

After an extended session of mass affection, they'd then all go and clear up some shit for a bit, just to balance it out.

There tends to be some riding at these events too of course, sometimes in the form of mini competitions. Like egg-and-spoon races on horseback. Overall you get a sense that these ponies spend an awful lot of time wondering what the fuck they did wrong in a previous life. It's an easy gig I suppose, but self-respect levels are pretty low amongst the nags.

It's at this stage that you might start noticing some odd behaviour — the naguine influence seeping into your child's life, outside of the lessons and structured horse activities themselves. Often small things, and usually nothing that would raise particular alarm, especially in isolation.

But as a pattern emerges, you should sit up and start to take notice. These are warning signs! Ignore them at your peril! As each stage is passed, your child is falling deeper and deeper into a lifelong dependency that they may never escape from. And just remember... it's probably you that'll be funding it, possibly forever.

Leading experts in the field of equine addiction have identified what they call the 'Dominant Eight Behavioural Tendencies', or D.E.B.T, as the key warning signs. Please commit them to memory and be on the lookout for them at all times.

1 - CONVERSATION

A conversation can be about a million different things, in theory at least. However, take careful note of what percentage of conversations between you and your child start to revolve around ponies. Sure, there's nothing wrong with discussing horses in principle if it's something they're spending time doing.

For example, if the following happens at the dinner table then I wouldn't be too alarmed.

Parent: How was your riding lesson today, darling?

Child: It was really good. We learnt how to make the horse walk slightly diagonally for some reason. Can we go swimming on Saturday?

No problem. A perfectly healthy, and satisfyingly brief, nag-related conversation between parent and child. However, read the following example carefully:

Parent: Would you pass the salt please, darling?

Child: Did you know that salt supplies two of the electrolytes that horses require. In addition to the sodium and chloride found in common salt, they also need potassium, calcium and magnesium, but in smaller amounts.

KLAXON ALARM! KLAXON ALARM!

When this type of conversation occurs frequently, you have to start being concerned. And when nags, numbnuts, horse sticks, salt licks and horse hotels make up more than 50% of all conversations, you have to be properly scared and consider professional help. I think we're at 97.3% currently in our household and all hope is lost. Our daughter is a full-on gee-gee junkie. Don't become like us.

2 - TIME

As discussed earlier, doing horse stuff can be time-consuming, even for a child. Lessons, shit-picking and horse stroking alone can take hours each day, but once you get to the competing stage then it really eats into their week. This is to be expected to some degree, but when you start to notice that the amount of time they're spending with their nag has moved from *a lot* to *excessive*, then you may have a problem on your hands.

Hopefully school will force your child away from horses for most of the weekdays, but there are the holidays to be wary of. Frankly, CC2 thinks of school as something she's made to do as a detour on the way to the horse hotel; it's a major pain for her and a complete waste of time that could be spent cleaning out shit.

When addiction has set in though, there's almost nothing else that the addict would rather do instead. If I asked CC2 if she'd like to go swimming on Saturday, then she'd look at me like I'd just tried to piss in the fridge. I can tell you now that she'll have a competition or a lesson, all day, because that's just how it is. And even if she didn't, she'd want to go and stroke the nag instead.

We once booked a family holiday and kept it a surprise from the kids. We actually fabricated some story about going to see relatives and bundled them into the car for the drive there. Once we reached the airport we yelled 'Surprise!' and gave them the exciting news that we were about to get on a plane to spend two weeks in an exotic beach-front location where we'd have a wonderful time together in the sun. CC2 started crying.

And that, my friends, is when you know there's a problem. When you can't bear to spend time away from the nag, even to have proper fun, then there must be something wrong. Seek help.

3 - TV & FILM

To most people, there isn't really much in the way of nag-related TV, perhaps outside of horse racing or an occasional bit of showjumping. It's not like you find horses wherever you look as you're channel surfing. But those who are addicted will seek out the horsey shit, and they know where to look.

If you're ever perusing your set-top box looking for something to watch and find yourself saying to your partner "Well that's odd.... I don't remember recording 23 episodes of a documentary about the role of horses in Ancient Egypt on the History channel", then you are quite possibly in a reasonable level of trouble.

If you have a subscription to an on-demand service like Netflix and you gave your child their own profile to stop a load of cartoon crap clogging up your recommendations, then take the time to log in as them occasionally and have a browse through their viewing history and any favourites or lists they've saved. If they've discovered some obscure animated series about the trials and tribulations of a load of pre-teenage girls who, weirdly, all live together at a horse hotel and have a load of nags with impossibly-coloured manes, then it's time to call your loved one down from their bedroom for a serious chat. And by the way, that wasn't a hypothetical example I just gave — that shit's real and CC2 watched Every. Fucking. Episode, of all 1,565 seasons, probably twice.

But the really serious shit is this: when your child learns the channel number of the dedicated horse channel on your satellite or cable box and taps it in as a matter of course when collapsing onto the sofa, then you're looking at a pretty serious-grade problem. But there's one thing that's even worse than that. When *you* know that number, just from seeing them tap it in so frequently. If you're in the UK and have Sky, then I can tell you that it's channel 253. And no, I didn't need to look that up. I just know. That's where the horses live on our TV. And that's also where the addiction lives.

4 - JEWELLERY

Probably more one for the addicted girls than boys, but there's nothing a horse addict wants to do more than spread the word of her addiction. You'd think they'd be embarrassed about what they've become, but no. Horse earrings are the big game in town here. If they're the little stud earrings, they don't even look good either, as they spin around, so the horse is as frequently upside down or pointing skyward as it is actually facing the right way up.

But this is no laughing matter, and laugh at your peril. Because this is a good, solid sign of a problem. It's not a guaranteed sign of a full-blown addiction, and a girl might have a whole range of different animals forced through her earlobes at different times, but the name of the game here is observation. Keep your wits about you and your eyes peeled. If the horses are indeed one of a whole range, and ones that only get worn occasionally, then you might well be OK. For now.

But when you have to pry those fuckers out from a pus-filled hole because they're pretty much rusted themselves in place then those alarm bells should be clanging away like... erm... alarm bells.

5 - DOODLING & DRAWING

People of all ages like to doodle. As adults, it's usually the sign of being in a really dull meeting, or being 87th in a queue of callers to your electricity company, because they're experiencing an unusually high call volume, despite your call being important to them.

But the more artistic amongst us like to actually *draw* stuff. Properly get out some pencils and fill a piece of paper with something thought-out and structured. Children seem to be far, far better at this, and it's one of the sad facts of life that children embody so much that we think is important in people, but which fades away in most of us as we mature into adults.

And that's all good and well, but when you find entire reams of paper with horse sketches on then you need to start a proper, controlled panic, and fuck all that stuff about fading artistic whatever as you get older and stuff. Remember that scene in *The Shining* where Shelley Duvall discovers that Jack Nicholson hasn't in fact written most of his novel but has just filled thousands of pages with the same single line, over and over again? Well, look how that turned out. With blood and axes, that's how.

Uncovering a nice little horse sketch might initially make you go "Aaaah!" and think about popping it onto the fridge under a comedy magnet shaped like a cactus which was a shit present from a friend visiting Nevada, but just take care at this stage. You might look back in a few years and realise that essentially what you were doing was normalising and even encouraging a burgeoning little addiction. You wouldn't find a pack of cigarettes hidden in a child's drawer and pop one on the fridge, would you? No, you would not.

And I'd like to make a very important point at this stage that applies to many of these warning signs, but none so much as the drawings... OK, take careful note of this because it's very important.

UNICORNS ARE ALSO HORSES.

Get that? To a child, a unicorn is just an extra special horse, possibly magical, possibly just rare, but potentially rideable all the same.

Don't get fooled into thinking that drawings of unicorns are somehow sweet and endearing and essentially unconnected with horses and any potential addiction. Nope. They're just a crack pipe decorated with glitter, my friend, that's all. Many an addiction has gone unnoticed in its early stages because the horses were all being represented with a horn on their faces and coloured an unlikely pink hue, but the warning signs are very real and shouldn't be ignored.

Stay Horse Wise. Stay Unicorn Aware.

6 - READING & WRITING

Reading is good. Children absolutely should be encouraged to read from a young age, and if your ten-year-old is getting through a decent-sized novel every week or two then well done you!

However. Note the contents of these books very carefully. You don't even have to read any of it, you can absolutely judge a book by its cover when it's a kid's book. And if that cover has a nag on the front and the word 'pony', 'horse' or 'foal' in the title then it's pretty clear what's going on here. Again, we're looking for a trend rather than just the odd outlier. A single pony book isn't bad for a child. Several from a series over a year, mixed with other books displays a healthy reading habit. But when they're getting through 50 a year and won't consider reading anything without a horse in it, then you might want to think about having a chat.

CC2 has actually moved on from this stage. She still reads a million pony series books, but has started reading other things too, now that she's a bit older. She reads the odd non-fiction book, even autobiographies. Yes, that's right. A history of horses and both Charlotte Dujardin and Carl Hester's autobiographies. Houston, we have a problem.

It's a similar story with writing. Again, what kind of parent would actively discourage their child from spending their evening or weekend mining their imaginations to produce an original piece of creative writing? When you start finding short stories and poems scattered on scraps of paper around the house, your chest initially swells with pride, and your mind is filled with visions of that lovely house in the South of France that your child's future royalties will inevitably buy you.

But then you start to notice a theme. And I think we all know where this is going.

Let the record show right now that I think CC2 is an amazing writer. Really. As mentioned above, she's a voracious (if mono-themed) reader and this shows through in her writing. She can write beautiful short stories of all kinds: adventures, thrillers, out-and-out horrors, or sometimes just poetic and descriptive verbal landscapes. I really do think she has an incredible talent, and I've already earmarked a few specific regions of the South of France that I have my eye on.

But to point out that there's a running theme should be unnecessary by this point. Being so skilled though, she's not always obvious from the beginning. Her stories don't ever start with anything so bluff as "There was once a pony..." or even "Jenny was in a terrible rush as she headed to the stables that morning". No. Her stories start with great opening lines and some mystery. It might be something like "The mist danced across the darkening shoreline as the lighthouse up on the rocks flashed for the very last time." And you're thinking to yourself, "OK, so where's the fucking horse?"

The story might progress a bit further, maybe introduce a hero, or a family or, I dunno, a mutant rabbit. It doesn't matter and there's really no need to fret. There'll be a nag along any minute now, trust me. And it'll save the day, transport the hero to safety or just generally be the entire point of the story.

Sometimes she might hand me a stack of pages for me to read through. And I've started doing a thing where I scan through for a split-second, trying to get an idea of how long it'll be before the horse appears. "Wow, not till page 2!", I might say to her with a respectful nod, and she'll usually correct me with a pointed finger, "Oh no, it arrives just at the bottom of the first page." Oh yes, so it does. Of course it does.

On other occasions, she'll tell us about a story she wrote at school and got a good mark for. "Cool!", I'll say, "Which kind was it? Hero, sport horse or transport?" And she'll answer with something like "The horse died at the beginning but came back as a ghost." "Ah, a new category", I'll say, impressed.

7 - ROLEPLAYING

Right. Now this is where things start to get seriously fucked up. We have two dogs, and we also have a garden. So far, so who-gives-a-shit. Well, this leads to a pair of classic warning signs, so read on please.

The first warning sign for me started a couple of years ago. I'd come home from work on a summer's evening and find two dining chairs missing. Following the trail into the garden would reveal a scene of some comedy. The chairs set up on the lawn opposite each other, with a stick balanced between them. And CC2 trying to teach the dogs to jump over it. Unsuccessfully. Basically, this involved her running towards the 'jump' at full speed, encouraging one of the dogs to follow, and then with a flurry of arms, legs and mixed signals, trying to get the dog to continue the trajectory in a graceful arc over the stick while she deviated to the side.

I've watched this scene unfold on countless evenings over the last couple of years, and not once have either of the dogs got even close to actually jumping over anything. They just run along behind CC2 and follow her around the obstacle, like any sensible animal, and at CC2's exasperated cries and gesticulations denouncing their failure, they just sit down and look up at her with a look that says, "Well what the fuck did you want me to do?"

Now, this might sound to you like something called *dog agility*. I've seen it on the telly at Crufts, and also at a puppy training class I took both dogs to where they learnt at a formative age how to fail at doing it. But it's not dog agility in CC2's mind. It's model pony jumping.

She actually told me the other day that dog agility is just horse jumping for nags who were born into the wrong bodies. And I'm pretty sure she believes this with all her heart. So if you have a potentially-addicted child and notice it spending a lot of time with the family dog, then look a little closer. Is she playing with the family dog, or with a very small, substitute horse? Mock if you like, but don't come crying to me in five years' time when you've just sold your car to pay for another pony.

There is a second stage to this one though, and there is no subtlety or ambiguity at all here. The child simply removes the dog from the equation and starts pretending she's a horse herself.

CC2 has spent many hours, many many hours, cantering around the living room, holding imaginary reins and making snorting and neighing sounds, looking like an extra from a Monty Python movie. From here she graduated to the doing the outside chair jumps herself, realising she could have more fun and significantly more success if she took over the jumping duties.

It turns out that you can even buy miniature horse jump sets, with little wooden stands and plastic poles that you can fit across them. We were given a set by some friends and CC2 has made good use of them. It's now not unusual to come home on a summer's evening, notice a full complement of dining chairs but hear whinnying noises from the garden anyway.

Following this trail will inevitably lead to a scene involving CC2, hands holding invisible reins nice and high, trotting around the garden before making a mad dash for the striped pole held about two feet in the air which she clears with a sort of pseudo-equine leap, while the dogs look on, as confused as hell and running around in circles, barking. Nurse! The pills!

If you don't think that this is a cry for help, then I think you probably need to question your own sanity.

It doesn't necessarily stop here though. In CC2's case, dressage being her particular poison, she encouraged me last year to leave the garden to grow long before mowing a miniature prancing pitch into it, so she could 'practise' her tests. Thinking this sounded like a proper revision aid (barking fucking mad of course, but reasonable in its own way), I even printed, cut out and laminated the letters and sellotaped them to wooden cooking skewers before staking them into the ground.

I'd assumed that she'd start walking her tests to ensure that she'd memorised them correctly. Obviously enough in retrospect, her aim was really to just hop around the pitch pretending to be a horse in a prancing competition rather than a showjumping one. Realising that I'd been duped and was just aiding and abetting her addiction, I naturally hid the letters and mowed over the whole thing, pronto.

8 - BIRTHDAYS AND CHRISTMAS

Buying presents for anyone can be a challenge, but it's a nightmare when you have kids. Toy fads come and go all the time, and woe betide the parent who buys their child *The Wrong Thing*.

I've found though that the last few years have been an absolute piece of piss in regard to CC2's presents. Family members will ring up a couple of weeks beforehand to ask us what she wants, and I always give the same reply now: "Doesn't matter at all, as long as it's for a horse, about a horse, or got a horse on it. Go wild."

This is entirely serious. All she really wants these days is stuff for the horse itself. Her birthday has now become the nag's birthday, except it doesn't know and doesn't give a shit anyway. But whether it likes it or not, the day after Christmas it's going to be brushed with a new brush, cushioned with a new numbnut, have its ankles decorated with new legwarmers and be lightly beaten with a new horse stick.

We can buy stuff for her instead of the nag as a last resort, as long as it has a horse on it somewhere. Could be a pen, could be a pad of paper, really doesn't matter. If we gave her a week-old cucumber with a horse outline scratched onto it with a rusty compass, she'd squeal in delight and hold it close to her chest with eyes squeezed shut. She's a right fucking horse simpleton.

So, on one hand you've got a major biannual problem completely and utterly solved and get to avoid even bothering to Google what this week's trendy toy is, let alone squandering all your self-respect by queuing up for the last ones on Christmas Eve. But on the other hand, you've got mounting evidence that your child is a hopeless addict who's given their life over completely to some kind of equine Satan. It's up to you to decide how to take this news. In all honesty, I was 50/50.

Once a nag addiction has been identified, what are the next steps? Well, there are three main options: firstly, you could just ignore it and let the addict carry on. Your take on this approach will probably depend to some extent on whether you're having to finance the addiction yourself or not. If the addict is self-funded then you're more likely to let them just get on with it, especially if they're an adult. But if you're the poor sucker having to foot all the bills then you'll probably want to ignore this option unless you're really rich.

Of course, the addict could be you yourself, dear reader! Your first instinct might well be to carry on simply because you're so addled with addiction that you can't see the problem for what it is. If this is the case, then I suggest you find a close friend or family member and ask them to be honest with you. If you really are addicted then it'll be pretty fucking obvious to anyone that knows you, and they'll be able to tell you pretty quickly. The conversation will probably go something like this:

You: I've been reading this *amazing* book about nags and stuff, and I'm a bit concerned that maybe I'm addicted and spending too much of my time and money buying *matchy matchy* shit and doing dressage competitions. I know I can talk to you and that you can be straight with me. So, honestly speaking, do you thin...

Friend: Yes.

You: Oh. Right. Thanks.

The second option is to try and wean the addict off the addiction, slowly. If you're the parent of an addicted child, then you could try reducing the regularity of lessons and entering fewer competitions. You'll have to be sly though, because a gee-gee junkie is hungry for horse time and they'll be very sensitive to any reduction. Keep your wits about you and play it cool. Also, lie a lot. You may have to get the trainer involved too, as they'll need to have a consistent story about their rare and exotic tropical disease that's contagious for 6 days of every week and limits their ability to give lessons on those days.

The third option is a full-on intervention. A complete stop to all horse contact and total ban on all horse-related activity. This is the nuclear option and comes with its own dangers. It's not for the faint-hearted but might be the only choice if things get serious.

We haven't actually done this yet; haven't pressed the big red button with 'de-horse' written on it. I'd like to, but CC1 won't let me. She goes on about how it's CC2's passion, her greatest love, how it makes her so happy etc. blah blah blah. Happy, schmappy, that's all I can say. What about me? What about all my money?!

That said, I do have some experience of what an intervention would be like as CC2 broke her collarbone recently and was therefore sworn off all riding by the doctor for a few weeks. Frankly, it took her to a dark, dark place.

I've never experienced it personally, but I imagine it's a bit like living with someone who you suspect is a serial killer. Or going mad in a really disturbing and cinematic way, like Jack Nicholson in The Shining. It got to the point where I'd catch some movement in the corner of my eye while having breakfast perhaps, look up instinctively and then catch a flash of pony tail and arm sling in my peripheral vision. Of course, I'd get up and follow, each corridor or doorway leading deeper into some dark and unexplored corner of the house, and at each turn I'd just catch that last glimpse of the outline of an 11-year-old girl as she disappeared into the shadows, and hear the high-pitched cackling echoing off the walls as I headed inexorably further towards some horrific discovery... like, maybe a vast collection of dead squirrels, or the entire LeMieux range of numbnuts, laid out in alphabetical order.

OK, maybe it wasn't quite that bad, but it was pretty bad. Basically, she was in a right fucking strop for the entire time. It wasn't a proper intervention either, because she was still allowed down to the horse hotel to do some horse stroking and shit-picking, and that would cheer her up. But only temporarily. I still hid all the knives and started locking our bedroom door at night, that's all I can say.

So, in terms of treatment there are options. But in summary, you're basically fucked. I've not actually experienced a full cure in an addict, to be honest. And sometimes, I think the addiction can lay dormant for several years while the addict appears to be in remission. I suspect this is the case for CC1; she rode a little as a child but never exhibited the symptoms of a full-blown addict, and hasn't ridden for decades. But I fear all this 'nurturing' of CC2's hobby/habit is just her way of getting her hit, like an ex-smoker walking really closely behind a stranger with a cigarette and breathing in deeply through each cloud of smoke.

I'm going to have to watch out for her too, I think. I've already started placing hairs between various pages of the *matchy matchy* catalogues that turn up at our house to see how much stuff she's looking at, and how expensive it is.

The watchword here for you all is 'observance'. Take great care to study the list of warning signs above, and keep your eyes peeled for any of the behaviours. If I can prevent just one child becoming addicted, then this chapter will have been worth it. It's taken, literally, over an hour to write now and I feel that's got to be worth one human life at least.

Don't fall into the trap that I did and ignore those signs until it's too late. And if anyone has any idea how to help me then for fuck's sake, let me know.

Nicotine and alcohol
With neat long lines of coke
Heroin and methadone
Bought from a dodgy bloke

Heroin and silver foil
Like Zammo in Grange Hill
Amphetamine and valium
Come in a little pill

Crystal meth and angel dust
Addictive stuff of course
But nothing quite prepares you
For the power of the horse

CHAPTER 2

How many horses do you need?

2

HOW MANY HORSES DO YOU NEED?

I would suggest that there's an incredibly simple answer to the question "How many horses do you need?" And that answer is 'None'. This is exactly how many I have myself and I'm quite happy about it. In fact, it's how many I've owned in total throughout my entire life.

I understand of course that I don't represent everyone who's reading this book. Quite possibly I represent nobody at all in fact, so I'd suggest that for you horse people there's a different answer. And it's 'One'. Not hard, is it? If you want a horse, get a horse. Simple.

But if there's one thing I've learnt from living with these awful horse people, it's that 'simple' is not a word that comes up a lot. Why have a nice colourful set of horse clothes when you can have 15? Why compete in a prancing competition nearby and get it over with in a couple of hours when you can spend several days attaching trailers to cars, driving back and forth to stables either with or without a nag in the back, loading up with hay, straw, car-loads of equipment and food and all kinds of other shit?

The following is an almost verbatim account of a conversation I had recently with CC2 while I drove her home from school. I think it says a lot on this issue.

CC2: You should sell this car and then you could buy me another pony.

Me: But you have a pony...

CC2: Yes, but she's for dressage. I need one for showjumping too.

Me: And your current pony can't do showjumping?

CC2: No. I need one for dressage and one for jumping.

Me: Ah, right, I see. So, in an ideal world you'd have two ponies?

CC2: No. I'd have four.

Me: Four?? But I thought you needed one for dressage and one for jumping?

CC2: Yes, but I'd need a second showjumper in case the first one got injured.

Me: Okaaaay.... and the fourth?

CC2: A project pony.

Me: OK. So what (*the fuck*) is a project pony??

CC2: It'd be for dressage, but one that I'd need to train up to a higher level. My current one is already at that level.

Me: Right. OK. I think I understand. So you need four ponies. You've got your basic dressage pony...

CC2 punches my arm, gives me an evil stare and speaks through gritted teeth

CC2: She is *not* a basic pony... she's an amazing pony!

Me: OK, OK. You've got your... *current* pony, a project pony, a showjumper and a spare showjumper in case the first showjumper gets hurt.

CC2: Yes. Except she's not a spare, she's just a second showjumper.

Me: In case the first one gets injured?

CC2: Yes. But she's not just a spare. I'd use her for competitions as well, she just wouldn't be quite as good as the first one.

Me: Right, so, in an ideal world you'd have four ponies?

CC2: Well, no. Actually eight.

Me: Eight???

CC2: Well, I also need a stallion dressage pony and a stallion showjumper, and a mare and her foal.

Me: OK, back up, back up. Why do you need a stallion dressage pony and stallion showjumper?

CC2: Because they have more pizazz.

Me: Pizazz?

CC2: Yes. Pizazz.

Me: I see. And what were the other things you said?

CC2: A mare and her foal.

Me: Of course. And why?

CC2: Because foals are cute, and I can cuddle it.

Me: You want a baby horse just so you can cuddle it?

CC2: Yes. But I'd also train it.

Me: Right. So what's the mare for?

CC2: Hmmm, you're right. I don't need the mare. I'd just need the foal. And I could train it to do both dressage and jumping.

Me: Oh right... so that's only seven then? You've

got your basic pony... ***PUNCH*** alright, alright...
you've got your current dressage pony, a project
dressage pony, a stallion dressage pony with more
pizazz, a showjumper, a spare showjumper...

CC2: Not a spare, just a second one...

Me: ... a *second* showjumper, a stallion showjumper,
and then a foal to cuddle and train for both
dressage and jumping.

CC: Hmmm... actually that won't work. The foal
can't be trained to do dressage *and* showjumping in
case she gets injured jumping and can't do dressage.
So I need two foals.

Me: (*under my breath*) Give me strength... OK. So.
You've got eight ponies again then?

CC2: Yes. Eight.

Me: Right. You've got your bas... *current* dressage
pony, a project dressage pony and a stallion
dressage pony...

CC2: Yes.

Me: And then a showjumping pony, a spare
showjumping pony...

CC2: Not a spare...

Me: Not a spare.... a *second* showjumping pony...

CC2: Yes.

CC2 and Me together: In case the first one gets
injured.

Me: Then a stallion showjumper with more
pizazz...

CC2: Pizazz.

Me: ...and then two foals, one for dressage and one
for showjumping. And for cuddling.

CC2: Yes.

Me: Right. So, just the eight ponies then?

CC2: Yes.

Me: Phew.

CC2: Well, and Valegro of course.

Me: Valegro?

CC2: Yes. Charlotte Dujardin's horse. Mum says he's not for sale, but all horses are for sale. You just have to offer enough money.

Me: I see. I'm not sure that if I sell my car I'd get enough for all that.

I once asked CC2 what her vision of heaven was. She described it from left to right with a wave of her hand across the breakfast table: "Pony, pony, pony, pony, pony, pony, funfair, pony."

I think the general equation here for how many nags a horse person needs is quite a simple one. If the number of horses currently owned is represented by the letter H, and the number needed in total is represented by the letter N, then the equation is simply $N=H+1$. In plain English, you always need one more than you currently have. In CC2's case, this is actually much worse and the equation you can derive from the conversation above is apparently $N=H+7$, but that's because she's young and just starting out.

This phenomenon is known as *Horse Acquisition Syndrome,* or H.A.S, and it's been identified by doctors as a pretty nasty condition.

There are various factors that contribute to a serious bout of H.A.S, some described elsewhere in this book. For example, horses come in different colours. Not many, but some. And like Pokémon, McDonald's Happy Meal toys and shit commemorative plates sold in the back of the Daily Mail, I think you're supposed to collect them all.

I'm not of course suggesting that horse people are all frivolous and superficial beings, obsessed by how pretty their nag looks in its matching clothes, but let's just say that I see the catalogues that get delivered to our house. They're two feet thick and just contain pretty horse clothes. CC2 already has too much *matchy matchy* shit just for one horse, but I know how her little mind works. She'll be thinking that that particular shade of *Chequebook Cherry* looks extremely fine on the current brown nag but, oh, wouldn't it also look rather splendid on a white one! Or even a black one! This is how it all starts, people...

Then of course you have the different horse sports entirely and I understand that they require different nags, as so eloquently described to me by CC2. I had a conversation with CC1 a while ago where she explained that the current nag was fine for dressage, but if CC2 was going to branch out into other disciplines that we should maybe start looking for a 'nice little jumper'. I naturally suggested *Marks & Spencer* but that didn't even raise a smile.

Having multiple horses then leads to all kinds of other practical and logistical issues, and therefore expense. Each horse has to be kept alive with food, put up in a horse hotel and transported to events. So you'll be at least doubling all the existing costs of a single horse, and it won't be long before you find yourself scouring the classifieds for a more capacious, and therefore costly, nag transport solution. I'm starting to get a light sweat on just thinking about all this.

The ultimate excess when it comes to H.A.S is of course in polo. This is a ludicrous way to get through horses, and at the highest levels, players basically switch onto a new horse every 5 to 6 seconds. It's ridiculous. They see the ball, run after it for a bit and then think "Right, well that's that horse knackered. NEXT!" And then do a fancy jump from one to the next one. Each player can get through over a thousand horses in every match. Crazy. A *string of ponies* doesn't sound so flash, but you have to think of it like a string of sausages, and before they get chopped up into a packet of 8. Just one, endless line of horses, disappearing off over the horizon.

Or, as CC2 might describe it... heaven. Once you add a funfair.

My daughter's new horse is a massive fat pet
But it slaughters resources and makes me regret
That I thought to encourage her love of rosette
So I sink ever deeper into financial debt

Now, of course she is special, that I'll never forget
And I'd never do anything to cause her upset
But her needs for these horses can never be met
If I bought her a second then she'd want a quartet

CHAPTER 3

What colours do horses come in?

WHAT COLOURS DO HORSES COME IN?

In the classic 1939 film *The Wizard of Oz* there was a horse in the Emerald City called the Horse of a Different Colour. Every few seconds, conveniently and suspiciously whenever the camera angle changed, its colour shifted from one garishly bright hue to another, passing through purple, orange and yellow. Sadly, in real life, horses aren't anything like as exciting as that and only come in a range of really dull colours. They also tend to stay the same colour at all times, in my experience.

Although the colours themselves are pretty boring, there's nevertheless a rich and wonderful range of terms to describe them. Much as I enjoy the poetry of these names, I can't help but think it's become unnecessarily complicated. So, in this chapter I'm going to attempt to demystify the naming process and, hopefully, bring a bit of welcome order and simplicity to the proceedings.

So, let's start with black. OK, pretty straightforward. If it's black then it's black. You can't really argue with black. It's just black — devoid of colour. And, simply enough, black horses are technically called... black. Excellent, we're all in agreement so far then. Apparently, black horses are actually quite unusual, but I've seen *Black Beauty* as well as endless Lloyds Bank adverts, so I know they're real.

I think if I had to have a horse myself I'd get a black one, because they look the coolest. Baddies in westerns usually have black horses, and baddies always have the coolest stuff.

Next is white, or shades of. Some nags are whitish, some greyish. Basically these are all off-white though, like you get with paint. Let's not waste time discussing various shades of grey, because grey is inherently boring. It's a dull afternoon, it's ageing hair and pallid skin. When you think of it like that, off-white actually makes it sound a bit more glitzy.

Right, then you have brown. And this is where shit starts to go wrong for me. I know what brown is, you know what brown is. But it's a word people seem a bit scared of in the horse world. Bay? It's brown. Sorrel? Brown. Chestnut? That's brown too. Liver chestnut, blood chestnut, mealy chestnut? Brown, brown and brown. You can put whatever word you like in front of 'chestnut', but I've seen actual chestnuts and they're all fucking brown. So, go wild if you like and have a 'sky chestnut' or a 'hazelnut chestnut' or an 'artisan organic free-range chestnut', it'll still be brown. Because chestnuts *are* brown.

It doesn't stop with the chestnuts though, does it? No it does not. Dun? Brown. Buckskin? BROWN! Seal brown? I think we all know the answer to that one, clue's in the name. Sometimes though, from what I've been reading, seal brown is apparently 'so dark it looks black'. Well it's fucking black then, isn't it? If it looks black then it is black. That's what colour is. If I painted my front door a shade of red that was so light it looked pink, then it would be pink. Not red. Honestly people, this isn't supposed to be hard.

But back to brown. Because it's always back to brown. As mentioned, there's yer basic bay (brown), and then all kinds of sub-bays. Bay silver (brown), blood bay (brown), dark bay (brown), bay rabicano? Bay what? Doesn't matter, 'cos it's just fucking brown. And it goes on..... bay roan, bay pinto, sandy bay. All lovely names. All. Just. Brown.

I've looked at a lot of pictures of horses now and have calculated that 74.7% of horses are brown. I actually think this may be a ploy in itself. CC2 has only got one horse... or so I've been led to believe. But it seems to have at least 3 different names depending on where it is. If it's hanging out at the horse hotel then it goes by one name, if it's competing then it's something completely different, and CC2 regularly refers to it as other things as well, though I think these are just affectionate nonsense. Am I being thick here? Am I being duped? I'm genuinely suspicious that there's some kind of plot afoot to sneak extra horses in and pretend they're all the same one. And it'd be easy too. Because guess what colour it is? It's brown. Like all the others.

I was browsing shiny new motorbikes in a showroom once, and commented on the very fetching shade of bright blue that one of the manufacturers used throughout their range at the time. The salesman told me that someone had been in a while back looking to buy a new bike. "Excellent," said the salesman, "which model were you thinking?" "I don't care," said the man, "as long as it's in that shade of blue". Turns out he was wanting to trade in his old bike for something new but didn't want his wife to know. His logic was that she wouldn't spot the difference as long as it was the same colour because she didn't care about bikes.

He actually got away with it too, for several months. She eventually noticed the registration was different though, and the game was up. But I fear the same may be happening to me. CC1 and CC2, plotting behind my back. "Let's get another horse!" "Excellent plan! But how will we persuade him?" "Oh we won't tell him. We'll just get another brown one in, he thinks they all look the same. You can even call it whatever you like, he's completely foxed by the whole naming thing anyway".

And, luckily for them, they still get to choose from 74.7% of new horses, so there's plenty of choice.

So that's three colours, and that's pretty much it for basic plain horses. Black, brown and off-white. It's nothing like as complicated as we've all been led to believe. The only exception is those that are more than one of these colours at a time, and this does happen. I like to term these all as 'confused'.

For example, there's skewbald, which is a brown and white two-tone, and piebald which is black and white. The latter includes zebras by the way. Also, Fresian cows. There's also a Fresian horse, but these are just black. All very confusing. There are also other kinds of different confused patterns, many with very funky names. Appaloosa, overo and tobiano for example.

But they're all just patterns using the three basic colours, I'm afraid, there is no *Horse of a Different Colour* out there. Unless unicorns really do exist of course. They don't, sorry, but CC2 is convinced they do. She says it's just that they're very good at hiding and that I can't prove they don't exist. She has a point there I suppose, and is cleverly invoking that age-old philosophical technique called *proving a nagative*. Also, unicorns are supposed to be white anyway, even if CC2 usually draws them as pink.

So, in conclusion, I think you'll agree I've shown that horse colours are nothing like as complicated or interesting as you previously thought. At the end of the day there are only actually three: black, brown and off-white. But mainly brown.

Copper dun, bronze dun, amber champagne
Chocolate palomino with a very pale mane

Then we have the chestnuts, liver, dark, honey
Cherry, blood and mealy too, the choice just isn't funny

Want to hear some more? Then I hope you have all day
So all I'm gonna do now is list a few called 'bay'

Sandy, wild and faded, silver, gold and copper
Mahogany and rabicano both sound very proper

Light and dark and sandy, all are very handy,
The roans and the pintos and the flaxens are just dandy

Silver dapple, buckskin, sorrel takes the crown
But the thing they've got in common is they're all just fucking
brown

CHAPTER 4

Are horses expensive?

ARE HORSES EXPENSIVE?

How do you make a small fortune out of horses? Start with a large one.

Boom boom! It's an old joke but entirely true in this case. Many hobbies can end up being expensive, especially once you start buying all the fanciest equipment and gadgets, but few are as genuinely nut-crushingly, eye-wincingly expensive as the naguine kind. You might think that your new set of golfing sticks made from pure unobtanium were expensive but that'll be fuck all compared to what you'll have to shell out when you let horses into your life.

So, exactly how expensive is horse ownership? Good question. Let me perhaps throw this back at you by asking three simple questions in return; how many vital organs do you currently have, how many are you actually using, and do you have a least favourite? Trust me, I've actually looked into this. Apparently, you can happily spare a kidney, a portion of liver, a lung, some intestines and an eyeball, and there's good money to be earned if you go to the right places. A fresh, healthy kidney can fetch up to

£100,000 in Israel, my research has found, and that could come in very handy indeed currently.

Basically, every aspect of owning and riding horses is expensive. The naganomics at play are simply not in your favour. The horses themselves are expensive to buy, they're expensive to run, they wear expensive clothes (for some reason), it's expensive putting them up in horse hotels, it's expensive moving them around from place to place and, on top of all that, everything you buy in relation to horses has some kind of secret Horse Tax applied on top. If you bought an apple and said it was for a nag it'd be twenty quid.

I found just the other day that CC1 had bought some salt for the nag, that came in a big tub. I found the receipt and it had cost about a million fucking quid. It was salt. In a tub. But for a horse. And it had a special name, like 'Equine Performance Salt' or some shit, like when they try to flog sugared water to runners by just using words like 'hydration', 'fluids' and even 'aqua' to justify it costing a fiver a litre. But it was just some salt. In a tub.

Owning a horse is like standing in a muddy field for hours on end, freezing your tits off and setting fire to twenties to try and stay warm.

Before you start worrying about all the associated costs of horse hotels, horse clothes, lorries and competitions etc, you're going to need to get hold of an actual horse. Luckily these are free. Hahahahaha, *slaps thigh and wipes tears from eye*

They're actually a bit like cars, in that you can get a really nice one for a shitload of money, or a ropey old banger for much less. The costs are actually pretty equivalent too, when you think about it. A few hundred quid for a proper old shitter and hundreds of thousands for the equivalent of an exotic supercar. In other words, a whole heap of money. You can even lease horses in the same way, because the up-front cost is often just too much to bear.

And much like cars, horses can go wrong in all kinds of ways, need regular servicing by a trained vet and usually require insurance to make sure that you don't have to sell the house when they go wrong. You'll be needing that house to sell later on anyway, as we'll soon see. They also need fuel in the form of food, and have consumables that wear out from contact with the ground. All very similar.

The main difference between cars and horses is that the nag can just decide to keel over and die at any point, thus leaving you broke, horseless and with nothing to sell on. People talk about cars 'dying' but they really just mean that they're broken and need fixing. They don't actually roll onto their backs and start biodegrading, and that's much worse.

In fact, it's fair to say that this event is a bit of a dead cert at some point. If you splash out and buy a really expensive car like a Ferrari, then you'll probably be out of pocket to the tune of at least £200,000. And that's a fuckload of dough by anyone's standards. It'll depreciate too of course, probably only being worth half that in a few years' time. But, if you were to look after it, keep it well maintained and in good condition, then the chances are that if you kept it for 40 years it'd be worth significantly more. Possibly several times more. Try that with a horse and you'll be deeply disappointed, I promise you.

Quite frankly, I've no idea why people spend so much on horses in the first place. I mean, I've seen them just wandering around in various parts of the country, completely wild. Pop down to the New Forest or Exmoor and they're fucking everywhere, ambling across roads and generally getting in the way. Surely you could just turn up with a lorry and entice one in with a juicy carrot? Paying for one is like going up to the Ikea till and asking how much for the little pencil.

If there were areas of the country where cars just pootled around on their own, completely driverless and ownerless, the second-hand market would crumble, I tell you.

OK. So let's assume you now have a horse to call your own. You've bought it, borrowed it or stolen it. Now the financial funfair's really going to start, and you'll be able to ride the merry-go-round of misery, the rollercoaster of recurring payments, the dodgems of debt and the haunted house of... well, scary shit.

Let's first assume you're going to want to sit on the nag at some point. Seems reasonable, doesn't it? There's only so much fun you can have repeatedly stroking it and you presumably want to actually ride the thing, sooner or later. Well, simple enough, just pop a saddle on, right? It's just a horse-shaped chair, can't be too expensive, surely? Well, you'd better sit down on a proper chair; this is one of the big ones.

I was told recently that we 'needed' a new saddle for CC2 and genuinely thought we were looking at a couple of hundred quid. I'd not been involved in the purchase of a saddle before as the current one was borrowed, so I decided to google them to get a better idea. I found a site that sold them and clicked on the link that said 'prices'. My heart stopped, and my body froze. Not because I'd seen a large and scary number, you understand. No, it was something far, far worse. Something deeply sinister that laid a rock of fear deep into the pit of my stomach. I saw...

no prices. Not a one. But in their place, I saw details of payment plans. 0% interest and monthly instalments. What the fuck? Was this a seat or a new car we had to buy?

If ever you're in any situation at all where you have to part with funds to buy something, you eventually reach a stage where you have to ask, "How much?" If the answer starts with any evasive words like "Well, the thing is, sir..." or "What you have to ask yourself is..." or "Would you like a seat?" then you know you're up shit creek, financially speaking. Whenever I find a shirt to buy and ask the sales assistant how much it is, I expect the answer of "That one's 35 pounds" or maybe "Let me check, but I think perhaps 39.99." A really good answer starts with "Oh, that one's in the sale I think." If instead the answer starts with "What price do you put on looking good?" or some shit like that then I know I've walked into the wrong shop. And I don't mean figuratively, I mean I've actually got lost and walked into the wrong shop. I don't go to those kinds of places on purpose.

After drinking in the lack of prices on the webpage, I then read the text that was sat alongside the payment plans. There was a lot of blurb explaining about saddle purchasing being a major event and something that needs careful thought before committing to, and some questions you should be asking yourself to be sure that you really, really need to embark on such a costly exercise. My mouth ran a little dry and my eye started to twitch a bit. These are not good words to be reading when looking at an impending purchase, not good words at all.

After a while, my vision started to return from its blurred state, and I'd stopped being deafened by my own heartbeat. I managed to steady my quivering right hand with my left long enough to move the mouse and click into a second website. This one had a link to its online store, presumably with actual prices, so I took a deep breath, partially shielded my squinting eyes from the screen with one hand and then... clicked.

JESUS FUCKING CHRIST! SHITTING NORA! HOLY FUCKING SHIT!

I was now panting uncontrollably, the startled cat had leapt off the sofa and the dog had come running in to see what the danger was.

I had seen the numbers. I had seen the numbers. These were significantly worse than the first website has led me to believe, even. I started crying.

The dog was now looking at me with his head tilted at 45 degrees like a dressage trainer and his stupid, vacant face was asking "wosswong daddy?" He looked around the room and saw nothing to fear. The room was devoid of burglars, other bigger dogs or even cats now. After a second or two, he sloped off and went back to sleep. Clearly dogs only have an understanding of a very limited range of dangers. He was right though — sadly the purchase of a saddle can't be seen off by a dog.

At this point, I was starting to wrack my brains to work out how we were actually going to afford this. There are all kinds of nag expenses, as you'll read, and having to stick my hand in my pocket is pretty regular event. Everything is expensive in fact, but most of the usual costs have been in the oh-for-fuck's-sake-just-take-the-fucking-card-then category. Saddle purchase is in the do-we-really-need-two-cars category. You may want to start googling for medical advice for surviving on that one kidney.

What's even more depressing is that a saddle purchase isn't necessarily for life either. Not only do the different equine disciplines require different, separate saddles, but the nags apparently change shape over their lives as they gain or lose weight or muscle, and so your shapeshifting pony may well need several saddles over a lifetime.

Are you scared yet? You should be!

Saddles are actually not the most expensive purchase, however, as terrifying as that may seem. No, the really bad financial shocks come when you need to start ferrying your beloved nag around from place to place. That purchase is so vast that it's actually justified its own chapter, so skip ahead to Chapter 9 now if you really want to scare yourself. I don't recommend it though, I'd put it off for as long as possible if I were you.

After transport and saddles, the costs do start to drop off a little. But that certainly does not mean you can afford to be complacent, because the bills will just keep on coming prowling up to your door, and they usually hunt in packs.

If I was being cynical, I'd probably suggest that the amount of horse-related shit you need to buy and store somewhere will probably entail you buying a larger house at some point, but I don't think that point would stand up in court, so I'm going to retract it. But bear it in mind. Being horse-mad and living in a small flat don't exactly go hand in hand.

Our house is like a showroom for nagaphernalia and I really don't know how we'd manage if we had to live anywhere smaller. It's everywhere: rosettes, nag magazines, test sheets, legwarmers, bills. Every flat surface has small piles of laminated charts that tell CC2 whether to go left or right after entering at A, and receipts that I've stopped looking at for the sake of my blood pressure.

The clothes dryer in the kitchen will be laden most

days with *caramel* this and *mustard* that, usually joined by some new shade I've not previously seen but have presumably bought unwittingly. And we have a chest freezer in the utility room whose primary purpose is apparently as a rack for storing *matchy matchy* shit and horse rigging on. It also doubles occasionally as somewhere to store frozen food, but you have your work cut out for you to actually prise the lid open. When you finally do, all the loose items like legwarmers slide off the top and disappear down the back, lost forever. I swear that if you looked behind the freezer you'd find about a kilo of dust and dog hair, 37p in assorted change, a set of lost keys and at least three individual, unmatched legwarmers.

I'm more than happy for my daughter to have a hobby of course, but I just wish it was one that wasn't so fucking expensive. Something like deep sea exploration, or space travel perhaps. I suspect part of the problem is the joint bank account I share with CC1. It's completely down the middle, 50/50. By which I mean that I put the money in, and she takes exactly the same amount out. Apparently, this is 'fair'. She claims it all goes on food shopping etc, but every time all the horse stuff gets washed and hung up, there's always a suspiciously new colour of numbnut on display, like Overdraft Orange or Visa Violet. They're addicts, I tell you. I barely have enough left at the end of each week to afford the wine that I need to drink in order to read my bank statement without screaming.

Regarding our household finances, I'm regularly faced with a practical issue. Do I try to ensure I'm always present to oversee purchases, or keep as far away as possible in the hope of preserving my sanity? It's a tough call and neither is particularly ideal. CC1 took CC2 off once to go and 'look at a horse'. My first question was,

"What the fuck does 'look at' mean?" I knew the answer of course, and it was 'consider spending your money on'. Sending CC1 off on such a jaunt with my credit card would be like sending Charlie Sheen off to 'look at some drugs' while making sure he takes an extra big spoon with him. It's just not safe. But then when I do go with them, it's often unpleasant and I have to watch my money sail away, like a paper boat of cash on a fast-flowing stream of misery.

We all went to the horse shop a few months ago, CC1, CC2 and me. I say 'we went' as if it was a kind of family outing, but in reality it was the two of them and my credit card that went; they just needed me to operate the car. I only went along with it so I could grimace at the prices and keep a beady eye on them with my card.

The horse shop is a terrifying place. It's large and filled to the brim with stuff. Most of it in a range of colours, all of it expensive. This is CC2's Mecca, where she can walk slowly along each aisle, letting her hand gently stroke the range of goods on the shelf a bit like Russell Crowe walking through those wheat fields in Gladiator.

Here you'll find a full range of all the things you never want to have to buy, but eventually will. The first time you walk into a horse shop as a new nag owner or paying relative, you'll probably gaze in wonder at the quantity of items and think to yourself "Wow, imagine owning all this stuff!" Well, the good news is that you pretty much will within a few years, and the bad news is that you'll be paying for it long after that. You think 87 different colours of numbnuts and matching legwarmers seems excessive? Well so do I, but it doesn't mean you won't end up buying them. It's an addiction, as I keep telling you.

On this particular visit to the shop, CC2 happened to

be lusting after a new hat. Now, much like with saddles, my uneducated assumption was that this couldn't amount to a hugely significant purchase. Painful, yes, but not pliers-on-the-scrotum agony. I look wistfully back now at my rather endearing naivety.

We found the hat section and I was directed by CC2 to the specific hat she wanted. Looked OK. A basic sort of naghat, sort of blueish plastic mainly. Can't have been more than 15 quid. I had one a bit like it in 1982 when I went through a BMX phase.

And then I saw the price tag.

JESUS H CORBETT! STAP ME VITALS, IT'S JUST A PLASTIC FUCKING HAT!

I had to walk away on this occasion and do a few laps of the shop to calm down. CC2 actually started following me around the shop, whispering the name of the hat brand at my shoulder repeatedly, to try and convince me subconsciously. It was like some kind of horror film, or a nightmare where you wake up and find someone's drained your bank account to spend on numbnuts.

Eventually I stopped and turned to face her. She looked at me with her big tear-filled eyes and begged me outright to buy her the hat. For the record, I don't mean to suggest that she was actually crying. I'm just pointing out that she's spent hours in front of the mirror, practising how not to blink for 5 minutes in advance of walking into horse shops. You don't know her, but trust me... she'd steal your kitten, your family jewels and your Take That CDs and sell them to gypsies in a millisecond if she thought she'd get the cash for some *matchy matchy* shit and get away with it. And then she'd do that no-blinking thing on you when you confronted her.

Anyway, naturally I said no. Sometimes I like watching

her face full of disappointment, just a little. And then she asked me how much her head was worth! Unbelievable! What a low blow!

So of course, I did what any loving father would do; I did the maths. I set up a spreadsheet on my phone and plotted the Total Cost of Ownership (CC2's, not the hat), her depreciation, potential revenue from all future prancing and charted it all against the cost of a top-of-the-range (but cheap-looking) plastic naghat, and I have to tell you... it didn't look good. So I had to break it to her that basic maths dictated her head was worth around £154, and that just wasn't going to justify a new hat.

On that occasion I got off relatively lightly and I just bought her a new horse stick, a lump of salt in rainbow colours for the nag (WTF?) and something else that I didn't understand. It could've been a lot worse, but it was enough for my fingers to quiver slightly over the card machine as I tapped in my PIN.

Later on that day, I thought I'd look up the horse hats online to see how bad it can really get, and I came to realise that even the ridiculous thing I was shown in the shop was nothing compared to what's out there. Some of the manufacturers actually have full-on hat configurators where you can customise every last detail of your hat and choose from a wide range of really horrific options.

You can decide exactly what kind of exotic creature's skin you want it covered in, whether you want crystals encrusted all over it, and in what colour. They're like a cross between Porsche's website and that shop with all the ice cream toppings. To be honest, I'm not sure whether to be appalled or to show begrudging respect, though I think it's somewhere in the middle.

Naturally enough I played around with one of these to

try and come up with the most expensive combination I could muster. It ended up being a bright pink shell underneath with the skin of a baby panda stretched over the top that had been soaked in a mixture of vintage brandy and mermaid's tears to give it a unique lustre. Sprinkled over this like Oreo biscuit crumbs were genuine fake diamonds that spelt out the words 'Ha! Sucker!' It was truly ghastly. And the price!

I wouldn't want to say what this concoction actually totalled, but I've owned cars that cost less. Some that were still in the warranty period even. Now, maybe nobody will ever actually buy such a thing, but it just goes to show what's possible. When it comes to naghats, a certain amount of restraint will go a long way.

I'd like to point out at this juncture that you've probably been reading this chapter for about 15 minutes by now and we've vicariously spent an absolute fortune already and yet have only actually 'bought' three items. You've now got a horse, a seat for it and a hat. This is so just the beginning.

The person doing the riding will now require a full complement of clothing for themselves, aside from the hat. In Western movies they all just wear jeans and checked shirts and seem to do fine, but apparently this isn't good enough anymore. At the very least you'll be looking at jodhpurs by the million, shirts, gloves, jackets...

The horse will also require decking out in all manner of clothes, and for all the different seasons. It'll need keeping warm in winter, keeping cool in summer and keeping, well, sort of a normal temperature in spring and autumn. This will require a huge range of rugs, blankets, gimp masks, boots and everything in between. And that's just to keep it comfortable; to compete in any of the range of naguine disciplines requires a whole new wardrobe either for practicality or as fashion dictates, and the same applies for the human. That expensive dressage jacket just won't do for showjumping.

So we've now got a horse, all decked out in horse clothes and saddle, with a human perched safely on top and both looking splendid in the correct fashion for whatever activity you wish to pursue together. Marvellous.

Is that it? No, it's not.

The horse will of course require somewhere to live now — you can't just dress it up and then forget about it like a dog at Christmas, you have to put it up and keep it alive with food and stuff. The whole next chapter covers horse hotels, so I won't give too much away now, but think of it like taking in an adopted child and giving them everything they need. For years.

There are also running costs to consider and budget for. Horses wear shoes for some reason I'm yet to fathom and these require buying and fitting by an expert. Regularly. Then there'll be vet's bills, and there's no NHS for horses. You'll be paying for the services of a highly-educated horse doctor and that's merely 'expensive' until something breaks. And then you're really fucked, financially speaking. Unless of course you were wise to take out insurance, which you really should do. Though it's expensive.

Nags also need basic daily maintenance; cleaning and suchlike. Now, I actually own two buckets for washing my car, and a sponge or two. I don't do it very often, but I like to know I'm ready for action for when the mood strikes. It last struck in 2015, I think. It's a bit like Halley's comet, it's a beautiful thing to see but it doesn't come around all that often.

This is nothing to the comprehensive kit of brushes, sprays and all kind of other utensils that CC2 seems to own to attend to the daily horse stroking that's apparently required. She's got a big box, possibly more than one, and it's full to the brim with pink plastic shit. I've literally no idea what any of it's for, but it's all nag-related and I think I paid for it all. I can assume the quality of the products is good at least. CC2 says that the horse shampoo she uses on the pony is far better than that for humans and she uses it herself. There's also some kind of conditioner or something she sprays over the nag's tail that she swears by for her own hair.

It makes quite an odd scene to watch though, whenever I'm dragged down to the hotel after school. CC2 will be standing on her pink box of products to get enough height so she can wash, spray and scrub the horse. Every time the nag gets a squirt of this tail shine stuff, CC2 twists it towards her and gives herself a quick blast too. I'm not sure if it's delightful or disgusting to be honest, but I suppose it's all just detergent. And frankly, it's pretty much the only time I've ever known CC2 to volunteer detergents coming anywhere near her. She hates showers and baths as it removes the *eau de nag* that she prefers on her.

Frankly, I suspect I could go on indefinitely about the cost of running a horse. I think it would become repetitive pretty quickly in fact, assuming it hasn't already. Just know that if you let horses into your life you may as well start smearing your paycheques with peanut butter and feeding them to the dog.

I'd like to end with a snippet of a conversation that I once had with CC2 over the breakfast table. I think this speaks volumes and pretty much summarises the whole, sorry mess.

> **CC2:** If I didn't ride horses would you have more money?
>
> **Me:** Very much so. We'd go on holidays and have nice things
>
> **CC2:** So, if I said I was going to give up riding horses would you buy me a present?
>
> **Me:** Yep. I'd pretty much buy you anything
>
> **CC2:** OK, I'm giving up horses.
>
> **Me:** Cool, what can I buy you?
>
> **CC2:** A better horse!

Buy a horse? But of course!
I could do without divorce

Want another? Buy its brother!
I can borrow off my mother

Need some hay? Let me pay!
When you need more then just say

Another bill? Hey, I'm chill!
Think I've got some savings still

New hotel? Very well!
I'll just find something to sell

Four wheel drive? Man alive!
Don't know how I will survive

Second saddle? Brain is addled!
Up shit creek without a paddle

10 tonne truck? What the fuck?
Think you're running out of luck

Another horse? It's run its course!
Think that now I'll take divorce

CHAPTER 5

Where do horses live?

WHERE DO HORSES LIVE?

Horses are basically wild creatures by design. Many of them live wonderful lives out in the middle of nowhere, wandering around naked and doing their own horsey thing. There's no school for them on Monday morning, no 9 to 5 and no carrying weird human luggage and pretending to enjoy jumping over stuff or walking in a weird diagonal way.

But those horses that work with us have to be put up somewhere. And that means special horse accommodation. And someone has to pay. It could be you, it could be me. Well, it's definitely me, I know that much, I just don't know whether it's you too. If you're currently nodding sagely and slightly ruefully though, then it probably is you as well. If you're not sure what I'm talking about then you're a lucky bastard. But if you look around the room you're currently sat in and see someone with a large glass of wine in their hand, looking blankly into the middle distance while their right eye keeps twitching slightly, then it's probably them. Be nice to them.

Horse accommodation comes in various degrees of

expense, naturally, starting from *really expensive* all the way up to *really really fucking expensive*. Essentially though, and unlike the complexities of, say, choosing which kind of horse transport to buy, the level of expense you have to face when dealing with naguine accommodation boils down to one simple question: how much horseshit do you want to clear up yourself? For horses, the expense of the accommodation is inversely proportional to how much faeces you have to deal with.

You see, just like with human hotels, the price of a horse hotel depends on what kind of service you expect to receive. There are three main levels of service, but the definition of these differs slightly from that used in human hotels. In these, there are star ratings that are granted based on the quality of the food, the cleanliness of the room and the location of the hotel in relation to local points of interest.

Your basic horse gives no shits at all about any of these things. Food quality isn't much of a concern when you only eat grass (dried or otherwise), the cleanliness of the accommodation means little when you shit and piss on your own bed, and proximity to local points of interest is irrelevant when you're driven by your own personal driver to anywhere you need to go.

So the nag itself is going to be reasonably happy with whatever hotel you choose to book them into. The cost to you comes down to that one simple metric; how much of its shit are you prepared to clean up yourself.

Pricing is essentially broken down into three different classifications: *full shitpicking*, *part shitpicking* and *pick it yourself* (PIY).

With *full shitpicking*, you need never experience the warm, cosy feel of fresh horseshit under your own fingernails. This is the premium option, the full board and lodging that, on one hand means that you're most removed from the everyday care of your nag and least likely to build that precious bond between horse and horse person. But on the other hand, it means that people are less likely to ask to be moved away from you if you go out to dinner.

You can sleep soundly at night knowing that some young fool is going to attend to your nag's every toilet need, make sure it's fed and watered and generally kept alive and happy, while you sit at home and order *matchy matchy* shit online to stockpile and take with you the next time you visit.

This is definitely the right option, by the way. Short of not having a fucking horse in the first place, this is absolutely and definitely the best approach. Do you know how many times I've changed the oil on my current car? None of course. When I was 18, I used to change the oil, carry out basic repairs (because my cars were always shit and needed repairing every week) and generally do everything that was possible without requiring the services of a paid professional. But then I got older, got a job and became an actual human and decided I'd be better off (and considerably safer) if I just got other people to do the job properly for me.

And so it's been a fair while since I changed my oil or bled my brakes or, frankly, did anything other than wash my car and top up the screen wash. What's more, my car doesn't need the oil changing every single day, and if it required daily care then I'd *really* get someone else onto the case.

The next package down is *part shitpicking*. Essentially this is the same as the *full shitpicking*, but purely on a Monday to Friday basis. So, you can attend to the commitments of a full-time job during the week, and then spend your weekends clearing out the shit and piss of your beloved nag instead of enjoying yourself, or spending time with your family. Your actual family I mean, not the equine kind.

PIY is the cheapest option and is basically board-only. The nag gets to stay in its warm and dry room but gets fuck all food or anything else, so you have to turn up every day without fail to both feed and de-shit it. This is the economy option and ideal if you don't have a job. But if you don't have a job then how do you afford the nag? Clearly you have time on your hands but not enough money to pay for *full shitpicking*. It sounds like your partner doesn't love you enough. Have a word after dinner, but for fuck's sake, don't bring me into this. I have enough problems dealing with my own domestic naguine issues, I don't want yours too.

There is of course, a Fourth Way. It's like the Third Way of 1990s political thought except one bigger and, y'know, even shitter. And that's the concept of keeping the nag at home with you.

Now, for the great majority of you, this is going to be a non-starter anyway. You need some kind of stable and enough land to let the thing graze, as I understand it. But just think, how amazing would it be if it were possible? No hotel bills at all, complete visibility of the nag at all times, instant access whenever needed and no break in that beautiful and wondrous bond between horse person and horse.

Well, I'm here to tell you now that that's a massive load of bollocks. If you take away any lasting message at all from this piss-poor attempt at a book it should be this: Do. Not. Let. A. Horse. Onto. Your. Property.

You see, horses are essentially very destructive. I mean seriously, look at them. They're fucking massive. And usually have special heavy-duty spades nailed to their feet. You can see where this is going, can't you?

Sure, if you're lucky/unlucky enough to own proper equestrian facilities then you should go for it. I mean, it would've been a pretty massive waste of money otherwise, wouldn't it? It's both CC1 and CC2's dream to have something like this. When CC1 spends hours poring over the ads on property websites, dreaming about spending my money, she gets more excited by seeing the word 'equestrian' than by anything else in the property description.

She'll tug at my sleeve with an "Ooh, ooh, look at this one! Look, it's got 12 stables and a walker and a school!" I don't really know what most of that means, except that we don't have 12 horses, we don't have £2 million and the kids already have a school. I do fear though that if I did have £2 million then we'd suddenly have 12 horses. And a spare school.

The irony of course is that there would've been a far greater chance of being able to afford a house with a proper stable if we'd never allowed CC2 to get into horses in the first place. Though that paints a pretty bleak image of owning a big house with an adjoining stable filled with no horses. Presumably it'd very quickly get filled with some other junk instead, like every other spare space in our house. Ultimately, we'd probably just start taking the bins out less often.

Stable ownership is definitely an important part of CC1's dream house, but frankly, I couldn't think of anything worse. I'm shuddering just thinking about it now. All that mud. All those flies. All those... horses. Eugh! It's the absolute opposite of *my* dream house that would be completely and utterly free of cracked concrete yards with drains, and manky old buckets everywhere. No, mine would have a massive underground car park, all white and spotlessly clean, and filled with an array of beautiful (and clean) cars. There'd be a nice wine cellar. And a recording studio. And an airstrip and hangar. But no horses.

Obviously, I've had to deal with the naguine way of life to some extent, but I like to maintain as much physical separation as possible. The deal between CC1 and me basically goes like this: here, take all my money but leave me enough for petrol and wine, and then take CC2 over there somewhere in the distance and do horse stuff together. I get roped in to offer moral support and driving duties etc on occasion, but in general, the further I am away from all the horse business and associated mud, the happier we all are. And so I'd really much rather not have to live with having a horse at home.

But, sadly, I do have some experience of letting these beasts onto our property. You see, we do (sort of) have a paddock. It's really just a small patch of land at the end of the garden, and when we moved in a few years ago it was basically a wild mess of nettles, thistles and other bad shit. But, slowly, I've tamed it. I can't tell you how many hours I've worked on that fucking piece of land because you'd laugh at me. Suffice it to say, it's not just been the occasional summer weekends; I actually took a week off work once just to spend time on it, and I had to hire powered machinery.

But, and here's the thing, I've turned that patch of scrubby land into my own little garden. I don't do much in it, mind you. 99% of the time is spent working on it to make it nice for the other 1% of the time, which will usually be when I have friends over and we sit in it and drink wine. But I secretly enjoy the endless 99% of mowing, mending the mower, picking up bits of wood, making bonfires, mending the mower, strimming, mending the mower etc etc. It's your basic manly stuff, working my land. I even have overalls I sometimes wear — and only partly for comedy value.

And so, on a summer's day it all looks pretty lovely. Well-mown, tidy, nice pile of firewood I manly chainsawed up and neatly stacked after a tree fell over. Idyllic. But this all went horribly tits-up a while ago when CC1 decided that the nag should have a holiday from the hotel and stay over at ours for a bit.

I was told that it'd only be for a night or two and as it'd been so hot and dry that there was no danger to the neatly-trimmed ground. It would also do a lovely job of nibbling down the grass, giving me a day off from mowing as the nag would just wander round, calmly grazing and generally chilling out and looking like a scene from a Constable painting.

That's not what happened of course because horses are ridiculous, paranoid and unstable creatures. So when I looked out from the kitchen window that first morning, I was gazing out onto a scene that reminded me not so much of a tranquil Constable painting but more of the Charge of the Light Brigade. It was a scene of pure carnage out there, a blur of brown horsemeat whirling around in tight circles, back legs kicking violently, clods of neatly-trimmed earth flying in all directions. FFS.

Clearly it got spooked by something. Probably a molecule of air or a blade of grass moving in the breeze. And it went spastic.

I saw CC1 rush off towards it in a panic and it was

eventually placated. After a little time it was finally dozing in the shade of a tree looking peaceful and bucolic, just like we'd originally agreed.

I went out there to inspect the ground and I can tell you, I was Not Impressed. It's amazing what deep holes a horse can make in the ground, quite frankly. Or maybe not, given there's a tonne of angry mammal stamping four metal trowels into turf as hard as it can, and at some considerable speed.

I tried to make some basic repairs, replacing huge chunks of earth back into huge-chunk-of-earth-shaped holes, but it was a complete mess out there. I'm sure in a few years it'll be fine again, but it won't be for a long time yet. The horse was sent back to the hotel where, presumably, the meter had been running all along, and I've reinstated my previous no-massive-land-mammal rule in the garden. I might even make a sign. I own a laminator.

So, please learn from this lesson and go for one of the rooms at the hotel instead; it'll all be much better for everyone in the long run. And don't weaken, even for a weekend.

The hotels themselves are odd affairs. I've had to spend time at quite a few of them over the years, in my official capacity as dogsbody. It goes without saying that I don't like them very much. It's mainly the horses that put me off, but that's probably unfair of me seeing as that's the whole point of them. I don't really like anything else about them either though, so I have a pretty balanced and fair view of things.

Firstly, I'm never really sure who's in charge. Whenever

I arrive as taxi driver, I find somewhere to park that's as clean as possible and, ideally, a fair way from the inevitable dung pile that'll be in the parking area, and my young fare will spring out of the car and disappear off somewhere. As I wander blindly around, I'll tend to pass various people, some adults and some children, usually girls. The adults are always carrying a saddle and will usually pass with a cheery "Hello!", sometimes with a strong European accent that I can never place. I respond in kind (without the accent of course), but never know whether they're the owner, an employee, a parent or are tending their own nags.

If other mothers turn up with their offspring, then they all swarm together and start chatting merrily. I can never tell whether they actually know each other or just respond to some kind of invisible signal, maybe pheromones, that triggers the reaction. It doesn't work on me though, or any other fathers it seems, and so we just stand around awkwardly, like we do when picking up the kids from school or when accompanying them to parties. If we make eye contact with each other then we have to make a sort of half-smile, half-nod gesture that's actually quite complex when you study it.

It initially seems to just mean "Hello", but actually covers all of the following:

- Hello.
- I'm the Dad.
- I assume you are too.
- I'm here entirely legally in my capacity as parent and/or guardian, I'm not planning to steal a child, I want to make that absolutely clear.

- Look, there's mine over there, you just saw me arrive with her.
- OK, that's all clear.
- God, we're such doormats, aren't we, driving our kids around!
- I'm not really a doormat though, I'm actually well respected in my professional life.
- Look, that's my car over there. It's pretty good, isn't it? Wasn't cheap as you can probably tell, so that clearly reinforces the professional angle thing I just mentioned.
- I've checked out your car too. Yeah, it's nice.
- God, I'd much rather be somewhere else.
- I imagine you would too.
- Somewhere manly, like watching sport or drinking beer in a pub. Or both.
- Ha, we should totally be doing that together rather than both being here in this stable.
- But not in a gay way. I mean, I'm completely straight. Look! Offspring! I produced that!
- But yeah, just as friends.
- Ah, well this is fun.
- I'll probably see you again some time, but for now I'm just going to stand over there a bit and maybe pretend to do something, or look for my child or check my phone even though we both already know there's fuck all signal.
- Anything really as this is a tiny bit awkward.
- I'm English y'see, social interaction with strangers isn't really my thing.
- Not yours either? Ha, yeah, cool.
- OK, well, see you then.
- Cheers.

- Bye.

It's amazing really that one gesture lasting a fraction of a second can actually convey all of that so successfully, but I can assure you it does. Women don't have that same skill, so end up actually talking to each other instead, for better or worse. We've had that need entirely evolved out of us, assuming we ever had it in the first place.

I once went on a weekend holiday with a mate of mine, and when I got back my girlfriend asked me what we talked about. I casually replied "Oh, nothing". Not satisfied though, she pushed for a better answer. "No really, I'm curious... what did the two of you actually talk about for three days?" I put my newspaper down and trawled my memory for an accurate answer. "Nothing. I don't recall a single meaningful conversation of any kind. We just discussed which pub to go to or whether it was time to get some food. Nothing else."

And it was true. Men don't actually need to talk if there's nothing to say. A quick nod covers most things most of the time.

So I stand around, trying to look natural and try to guess who's who. I've been doing this for many years now at various hotels and have never really got anywhere with it. But I've come to one conclusion and that's that they're all actually owned and managed by dogs. There's always a dog, often several, and one of them usually seems like it's in charge. They have a certain swagger, a certain proprietorial confidence.

In most cases when you meet a strange dog at their home, they'll react in one of a few standard ways. They might be the protective kind and start barking at you. Sometimes they do that conflicted running forward and backwards thing while barking as if to say "Who goes there, state your business, don't mess with me! But fuck, I'm so scared, be nice to me! I'm not really scared actually, I'm big and tough! Hear me roar! Oh no, some wee came out..."

Other times, they're openly friendly and submissive, and just want a good tummy rub or scratch behind the ears, or will drop a ball at your feet because they want to play.

But these stable owner dogs are different and have an aloofness and maturity about them. You can tell which one the owner is because they'll come and see you on your first visit. Not immediately of course, they have important paperwork to deal with and aren't to be rushed, but after five minutes or so they'll come and find you. You'll catch them out of the corner of your eye making a beeline straight for you — not running, that would be childish, but not dawdling either.

They come over and stop a few feet away, then look you up and down dismissively. They don't say anything of course, they're dogs, but I get the impression they're checking you out to see if you can pay the bills. They'll often have a quick look over to see what car you drive, just to make sure, and then after a last lingering and impassive stare, they turn around and wander off again, back to work.

There are often other animals too; sometimes chickens, maybe a pig, usually cats, probably swallows darting in and out of the open stable doors. It's like a scene from a Disney cartoon, just with a much richer smell.

There are various other parts of the hotel, some obligatory and some optional, depending on how flash it is. There's always a Tacky Room, for example. I think it's called this because of all the pink ribbons and plastic 'diamonds' stuck to all the horse rigging. This room will house all the naghats and horse sticks, saddles and other nagaphernalia. Sometimes each rider will have their own hook or shelf to store their shit, labelled with their name. And usually some stars or hearts around it.

Then there are the functional areas for training and the like. I'm a bit vague about these, but there's generally some kind of practice pitch covered with sand and cut-up car tyres where you can do prancing or jumping over things.

And then there are the fields where the nags hang around when they're not in their rooms or doing activities. These are basically like outdoor equivalents of the day rooms you get in old people's homes. The nags stand around staring into the distance and reminiscing about the good old days when the grass was that much greener and young horses had more purpose.

So, there you go. You have the three options to choose from and it's horses for courses; pick the one that best suits your needs and how skint you want to be. If you want my opinion though, which you probably don't, you'll have chosen the *full shitpicking* option and so will be at home instead, sipping wine in front of the TV and talking to human people about something other than horses. I'd recommend spending as little time as possible at the hotel. Dreadful places.

I currently live in a very nice place
Where there's plenty to do and there's plenty of space
The waiters they send are polite, never rude
And they come every morning with lashings of food

If it's cold then they dress me and put on my coat
I've a choice of these ranging in thickness, please note
If my diary is clear then I'll go for a stroll
To a field with a view where I'll start with a roll

For the rest of the day I might take it quite slow
Spot of lunch, then a doze; life is tiring y'know
I may seek out some friends for a nice little chat
The time drifts away when we're chewing the fat

As the evening falls I retire to my room
If my coat needs a clean then I'll send for my groom
And also a brush if my hair has got messed
It's very important a chap looks his best

As I wait I may take a quick pre-dinner drink
And in fact, after that, yes! Another, I think
With the long day I've had it is quite well deserved
Then the waiters arrive. At last! Dinner is served!

Once I'm perfectly full then it's off with the light
And exhausted, I'll take to my bed for the night
I have to admit that I live rather well
In my excellent, luxury, five-star hotel

CHAPTER 6

Are horses dangerous?

ARE HORSES DANGEROUS?

When looking at the potential danger of any given sport or activity, the most scientific approach is of course to study the data. Search out the statistics, trawl through them and carefully compare them with other activities, taking care to provide like-for-like analysis so that you can find an accident rate over a given number of hours, or per capita of the population for example. Apply this approach correctly and you can derive an accurate indication of the relative danger and make a fair assessment as to where it stands compared to other activities.

Or, you can just take a look at what's going on and use some common sense. Applying this model to the question, I've come up with an answer I'm happy with. Of course they're fucking dangerous.

What we're dealing with here is taking a tonne of heavily-muscled, semi-wild, 6-foot tall animal that can run at up to 40mph, strapping yourself onto it and then seeing what happens. This can go wrong in about a million different ways.

What's more, they can bite like a shark and kick like Bruce Lee wearing metal shoes so you're not even safe when you just happen to be in the vicinity of one. Frankly, not only do I avoid riding the things, but I like to keep about 20 feet of clear distance between us at all times. I'm not a big fan of any part of them and from any angle. Remember, the front bites, the middle bucks and the rear kicks.

The simple act of getting on a horse and riding it is inherently dangerous. Here's what you have to do. Find an area of hard concrete, walk up a miniature flight of stairs and then heave yourself onto the back of the thing and try to keep balance on top of it. You can fall off and do some pretty reasonable damage to yourself just at this stage before anything's actually gone wrong — that's just gravity at work.

Now you need to try and make it go somewhere or do something. Over the millennia, a system of code words and little noises have evolved that together comprise a sort of miniature language that humans use to communicate with their equine chums. Unfortunately, nobody has ever bothered to ask the horses what works for them, and so much of it seems to fall on deaf, if twitchy, ears. This is where it all falls down for me and crosses the boundary from 'sensible' to 'dangerous'.

If I were to get into a car for example, or a boat or a motorbike or a plane or jet ski or quad bike or tank or crane or train or anything else with an engine and mechanical controls, then I'd push whatever levers and buttons were made available to make it do what I wanted it to do. With enough training and practice I'd be able to make it do *exactly* what I'd want it to do in theory, pretty much every time. On many occasions now I've witnessed people get onto a horse, make the little clicking noise in their mouth that everyone has deemed most appropriate, say "Walk on!" or some such and then watch as the nag either walks backwards, turns in a circle or, most likely, does fuck all.

From what I can see, the horse doesn't really give two shits what you say to it or how well you can do the clicking thing, it's only really when it's given a bit of a kick or a yank that it knows what's happening and then *may* consider heading off. This is basically the equivalent of trying to light a barbecue by following all the instructions: positioning firelighters carefully and trying to light the bastards with some kind of safety lighter before eventually just dousing the whole thing in petrol and flicking a match onto it from a distance.

Now I'm more than happy to make a dangerous explosion in a BBQ in order to burn food, but I wouldn't then strap myself to it and roll down a hill with no brakes. In the words of Duncan Bannatyne from *Dragon's Den* — I'm oot.

Of course, despite having minimal control over the nag and it not even coming with so much as a steering wheel, at least we can all relax because horses are well known for being so reliably placid and completely calm given any kind of shock or unusual situation. Are they fuck. This is the thing that really makes me never want to ride the things — the fact that they go absolutely mental for no good reason. I think they tend to be good reasons to the horse, which is all very well, but that's just not enough for me.

This is known in the trade as spooking, and doesn't

require anything as scary as an actual spook to kick things off. Something like an ant walking faster than usual, a distant cloud shaped slightly like a kettle or the memory of some bad weather a few years ago appear to be enough to cause a good spooking. And when the horse spooks then it goes fucking mental, or GFM.

CC2 was doing some prancing practice at the end of last winter when there were a few small piles of slushy snow still left over from the previous week's snowfall and this was enough to trigger a proper bout of GFM. The theory according to CC2 and her trainer was that the horse was suspicious of the snow mounds as they were new, and therefore could possibly harbour some new and unknown evil beings of some kind. Consequently, there followed a series of violent kicks with CC2 holding on tight as it tried to kick out at these invisible demons.

The thing is, that's fucking nuts. Properly mental. If a human person started thrashing out violently because of imaginary demons then they'd be sectioned, and rightly so. Why horse people deem it fun to strap themselves onto a demented, paranoid, hallucinating animal is completely beyond me. I've played Buckaroo, I've seen what can happen.

If I was to go shopping for a car and found one I was interested in, the following conversation with a salesman is pretty word-for-word how I'd expect it *not* to go.

Me: So, this car... tell me a bit about it.
Salesman: Well, it's the 2013 model, done 28,000 miles and with just one owner.
Me: Sounds good, anything else I need to know?
Salesman: Not really, no. Always been garaged, no

scratches, tyres in good condition. Oh, and when you drive past small piles of melting snow it tends to leap into the air by about 6 feet, open the doors and try to violently eject you…

Me: Sure. And full dealer service history?

You see, the last line would actually be "WTF??! Are you fucking mental? Constables! Arrest this man immediately! Better still… nurse! Sedate this man! Fetch the orderlies with the giant comedy butterfly nets!"

Of course, some horses are more likely to GFM than others. Some are particularly nuts and neurotic while others, in theory at least, less so. Really safe horses are known as being 'bombproof' and that's a term I've heard quite a lot when dealing with ponies for CC2 or her young friends.

I don't want to have to state the obvious here, but when people make 'bombproof' military vehicles or bank safes or whatever else, the term is defined by the fact that they've actually tested it next to bombs going off and it, y'know, survived intact. In the horse world it just means 'It's generally been OK up till now when somebody's spoken quite loudly nearby'. That is *not* the same thing.

Imagine that being the definition used by the military. "Here we are then, General. May I present our new FT-656 bombproof tactical reconnaissance vehicle." "Outstanding, Major, that looks like a fine piece of equipment. And exactly what explosive force can it withstand?" "Explosive? Oh god, no idea. We didn't think to try that. But someone opened a can of Coke literally right next to it last week and it was basically fine."

You know how people always say that their dog

'wouldn't hurt a fly' just before it eats someone's head off? Well this is the same thing. It's just an opinion you have based on your own, massively-prejudiced view of how nice the animal seems to be, but it hasn't so much as been asked what it would do in a given situation, let alone undergone a full psychological evaluation. Or been tested near a bomb.

CC2's last pony was 'bombproof'. Come round some time and I'll show you the photos I have of it on its rear legs, with CC2 hanging on for dear life! I think on that occasion it was spooked by the dressage letter "K" being a slightly different font than the rest.

So, from my perspective, simply sitting on a nag is dangerous enough. But the thing with horse people is that just walking around on a nag and trying to stay upright isn't actually enough for them. No, at this point they start wondering if there's anything nearby to try and jump over, or an area where they can see how fast the horse can run or, sometimes, both at the same time.

This is just looking to try and get hurt now. Do some horse stroking if you really feel you need to, but let's not go asking for trouble, eh?

Dressage isn't so bad in terms of danger. I mean, given the delicate nature of the nag's nervous system there's always a risk that it'll GFM just for the fun of it, but generally speaking all you're really asking of it is to go for a nice little stroll, albeit not always in a straight line.

Once you get to jumps though, things start to go wrong. First of all, you have the physical issue of hanging onto the thing while it glides through the air, but that's assuming everything actually goes perfectly to plan. The horse might well have an entirely different take on the situation and decide that the jump isn't for him after all.

Here we get into the physics of momentum. If the horse is running along at 20mph and then suddenly decides to stop, then physics dictates that you'll probably make the jump after all and still at 20mph. Just not necessarily with the horse under you. No, at this point you start to do a rather fetching Superman impression.

That part is actually fine and completely painless. It's the stopping quickly at the ground that hurts. And you know what I said earlier about horses kicking like Bruce Lee with metal shoes on? Well, now you're on the ground next to the horse and it's possibly an unhappy horse at this point. This is not a situation you really want to be in.

There's only so much that experience and skill will get you through this as well. Ultimately, if the horse is very polite and insists that you go first, there's not a whole heap you can do about it, and more so the faster you're going. I believe there's an expression that's relevant here: "The better you ride, the harder you fall. Beginners fall off. Good riders get launched." Quite.

Technology is starting to come to the rescue however, and you can now get riding jackets with built-in airbags. If at any point the horse decides you should get off and walk, the cord attached to the saddle is pulled and the airbag deploys, providing you with a soft, enveloping cushion of air, ideally before you hit the ground.

I saw this happen recently for the first time and have to confess that I didn't know about the jackets and was a bit confused as to what was happening. All I saw was a horse GFM, the rider fling into the air and then the horse sort of wheeled around with a jump as the airbag went off, possibly startled by it. There was a quick puff of smoke and a loud sort of 'Pffft!!' sound as the jacket filled with compressed air, and I have to admit I actually just thought it was a particularly impressive horse fart.

The question you have to ask yourself at this stage is this: if an activity justifies wearing your own airbag, is it perhaps a bit dangerous?

Course it fucking is!

Going for a quick ride
On my favourite little mare
It's just a little hack
To feel the wind blow through my hair
We're going rather quickly now
Much faster than I'd dare
I hope I don't come loose
And end up flying through the air

CHAPTER 7

What do horses wear?

WHAT DO HORSES WEAR?

Now, this might seem like a slightly odd question for those of you not acquainted with our equine friends. I mean, they're animals aren't they? They come with all the clothes they need built-in, surely?

To expand on this point further, we currently have two dogs and two cats, on top of the two children (not literally on top of, though they often are). CC1 is always banging on about getting more; she's one of those people who melts as soon as she sees a cute puppy or kitten and invariably turns to me with big, wide eyes and asks "Oooh, can we?" And I always look at her lovingly, smile sweetly and say "No". I have a strict household rule of only two examples per species at any one time, a bit like Noah. She's always welcome to any new cat, dog or child she likes, but she has to choose which from our current pair of that species to kill. It's basically the classic *one in, one out* policy, like keeping the fridge full of beer at a party.

I've suggested on many occasions that if we killed CC2 then we could make a cheaper child as a replacement — one whom we'd carefully shield from horses during its formative years until deemed safe from their lure. She's reluctant though, sadly. Tempted, but ultimately reluctant. She's less fussy about the cats though, I have to say. If we see a cute kitten that she wants to keep and I ask her which one of ours she's prepared to drown, she will often actually give me an answer. Usually it's the one that's shat in the bath most recently. Little bastards.

Anyway, we have two dogs and two cats. And if I look out of my window from where I'm sat, I can see two pigeons, a blackbird and a squirrel. And if I go outside for a short walk, I'll find a field of sheep and another with a few cows in. And what do they all have in common? I'll tell you what. None of them are wearing fucking clothes.

Horses too come fully equipped out of the womb with a nice coat that'll see them through most weather situations, and nice sturdy feet for walking through fields, but there are other reasons why they might need extra clothing. Mainly it's so that their owners can dress up their beloved nags like dolls. It's like a giant-scale version of the game Buckaroo — these poor animals get bundled up with layer upon layer of accessories until they finally have enough and kick out. And then you have to reset them and start again. Or maybe that's just Buckaroo. I'm not sure how actual horses work.

So, what is it that they actually wear then? Well, firstly of course there are saddles. These aren't technically clothes of course, but more a chair for the human. Just much more expensive. To ensure cost is kept to a maximum, these have to be custom-fitted to the horse as well as be a good fit for the rider. Also, they come in different styles, with each horse sport requiring a different kind. In other words, you're entering a world of financial pain just by looking at a saddle.

I was told by CC1 recently that CC2 would probably need a new, second saddle soon as she wanted to do more showjumping as well as the dressage. When I asked what kind of saddle she currently has, I was told it's a *General Purpose* saddle, and therefore not really suitable for both dressage and showjumping. I continued to stare at her for a full ten seconds after this, with a slight sideways squint, hoping that she'd see the irony in what she'd just said, but she didn't. I think the point here is that there is such a concept as a *General Purpose* saddle, but these are only suitable until such time as you find someone you can con into buying you at least two 'proper' saddles to use instead.

And the saddles aren't simply expensive on their own either. Oh no. They have to live in lovely, fitted bags and if they're to be transported around then they have to be be stored on special horseback-shaped stands that look like enclosed litter trays. The only benefit of these is that our cats actually live in ours at night.

You can't simply stick a saddle on a horse though, that would be too simple, and not expensive enough. You have to have a special blanket, called a numbnut, that sits under the saddle. This has two main purposes: firstly, it's designed to look pretty, and secondly, it can be used as an area to proudly display the logos of your sponsors. And by 'sponsor', I mean an uncle's pet shop or similar. Whoever last gave you twenty quid for some straw, anyway.

After the numnbut you have legwarmers, like the dancers used to wear in *Fame* in the 80s. (If you're under 40 then check with your mum for the cultural reference). These are basically long strips of coloured material that come rolled up in little plastic pouches, just big enough to fit into when new, but just small enough that you'll never get them back in again if you try. Like tents. These can then be laboriously wound around each nag leg to make the horse look particularly natty while out on the horse pitch, and then laboriously unwound again afterwards before being chucked in the back of the car.

There appear to be three conflicting schools of thought as to the physical effect legwarmers have on horses. The first is that they warm the tendons, which is good for the horse. The second is that they warm the tendons, which is bad for the horse. And the third is that they do fuck all for the tendons and the horse just wonders why it's being made to wear socks.

If legwarmers aren't heavy-duty enough for you, then there are also shin-pads like footballers wear. These are a bit more practical than legwarmers, and come in various degrees of protection, depending on how much you're planning to off-road your horse. But fear not! Practicality doesn't come at the expense of fashion and you can still buy even the most rugged option in a range of colours to suit your nag's look.

Next up are gimp masks. It all gets a bit sketchy here and I'm not really sure what the deal is, but some horses get to wear these things which make them look a bit like Mexican wrestlers. I assume it's just to make the nag look really badass and to intimidate the competition with. They come in a variety of designs; sometimes they just lightly cover the eyes and top part of the head, like a Batman mask, but other times the entire face is shrouded. In mystery.

Some are quite stylish and look more like the nag is off to a masked ball rather than a gimp party, but others are essentially just bin bags cable-tied over the head and look more like a kidnapping attempt. It really all comes down to how fashion-conscious your cool mule is, and also what kind of party they're going to later.

My favourite thing about these is that sometimes there are little cut-outs for the ears to spring out of, but other times they have full ear-gloves on them. You have to ask the horse which style they prefer, but remember to do this before you put the ear-gloves on so they can still hear the question.

Rugs are big business in the naguine world. You want rugs? Oh, we have rugs. We've got a rug for every occasion, like Donald Trump. There are stable rugs, travel rugs, turnout rugs, fly rugs, cooler rugs and exercise rugs, under rugs, over rugs, Wombling free.

If you say 'rug' to a non-horse person, they'll just picture a basic, rectangular piece of material, probably made out of wool and used to throw over something or lay down on the ground to sit on. A very straightforward proposition. But to a horse person, a rug is the answer to almost any horse-related issue. Is your nag too cold while it's in its stable? Then you need a stable rug. Is it too cold while standing outside? Ah, then you need a turnout rug. How about while travelling between stable and turnout? That's a travel rug. But what if your horse is actually too hot? Then you need a cooler rug. Outside doing light exercise but bothered by flies? A fly rug. And so it goes on. Whatever situation your horse might be in, there's a rug for that.

Of course, that's just the basics of the different rug types. They all of course come in a range of materials and colours too. And prices. If you don't love your horse very much, then you just buy some dull conventional rug in a plain colour. BORING! But if you really love your horse and want to keep up with all the latest in RugTech then you need to splash out on an anti-bacterial highly breathable and waterproof, UV-protected 3D-ducted tight-weave sports mesh performance fabric, with a patented anti-static memory foam fleece-lined inner with neoprene wither pads. In tartan. Like it? It's yours for the low, low price of a million pounds.

The very best and most expensive rugs of all are the magic ones. Sorry, *magnetic* ones. These are basically your standard rug with fridge magnets sewn into them at various points. The theory here is that the magnets exert a powerful force that aligns all of the money in your wallet into a single stream straight to the manufacturer. And they're very good at this. Sadly though, they're fuck all use for anything else, although you can attach shopping lists to them.

Essentially, you'll need to get yourself down to *Rugs R Us* and buy about ten of the fucking things for every rugging occasion. And don't forget the rug care aisle, where you'll need to stock up on the various cleaning solutions, sprays, brushes, waterproofers, conditioners etc etc. And then, presumably, spend hours actually using them to maintain and clean your rug collection. Enter the world of rugs and you enter a World of Pain.

So after all this rug shopping and expense, what does the horse actually look like in these garments? Pretty cool, you'd think, in such high-tech and trendy, designer gear. Well no, not usually. What you actually end up with, after you've rugged up your horse good and proper, is a horse in a bag. I've seen them standing around in the paddocks at the hotel, presumably wearing a *paddock rug* or a *Thursday afternoon rug*, and they look like they've got a duvet duct-taped around them. I always think they look like they're about to be posted somewhere. Add a gimp mask and some leg warmers, glue on a giant stamp and scribble 'FRAGILE' down the side and you're good to go.

The rest of the stuff you attach to a horse is basically the rigging. There's a tonne of leather straps and buckles that combine in various ways to hold things on, hold things up and hold things together. If it sounds to you like I'm being vague and skirting around the subject, then you'd be right. I've fuck all idea about how any of it works. It looks complicated. All I know is that there's a lot of it to get ready, a lot to strap up and a lot to clean afterwards. Also, it's quite heavy when you have to hold it all outstretched for ages while your child hoses it (and you) down after some prancing practice.

The only thing I do know about rigging comes from watching a particularly unpleasant episode when CC2 was competing and forgot to buckle everything together properly. Everything came loose and started to slip. She fell off. And that's bad. Falling off leads to a shit score and inevitably an even shitter drive home with a moody rider. The horse doesn't give two shits, mind you, and in this case just stood around, casually admiring the sky.

The last item of clothing is technically just part of the rigging, but it gets a special mention as it's deemed to be, well, special. It's called a horse tiara. This innocuous strip of rigging goes across the horse's forehead and is hugely important as it's where the rider stores and displays all her tackiest and shiniest shit. If a magpie was ever to get into a horse hotel and give it a good ransacking, it'd make off with every tiara in the place and would build a nest so shiny and sparkly that it'd never be able to get to sleep.

These can be decorated with simple patterns of coloured cotton woven around the leather, or made as flashy and garish as possible with genuine fake crystals.

Usually though, they're covered in cheap plastic beads and metallic sequins, puked up all over the thing in their hundreds. It's even possible to design your own, so can have whatever custom tackiness you like emblazoned across your nag's forehead. This is why they're stored in the Tacky Room. And it's very important that it's locked at night to keep all the magpies out.

From where I'm sat now, near the end of my years
I can look back with pride at my lengthy career
It wasn't so easy, back in the day
We lacked the things you take for granted today

Young ponies these days, they just don't know they're born
When they tell of their comforts I stifle a yawn
'Breathable' turnout rugs? Hay from a steamer??
Why, back in the day they'd have said you're a dreamer!

We were hot in the summer and the winters were cold
If we moaned and complained then we simply got sold
Rugs with fleece linings? Little gloves on their ears?
My god, they're so pampered, the poor little dears!

I see them all now as they're going to shows
We wanted to win but they just go to pose
They sit in huge lorries while their owners brew tea
With their safety ensured by the CCTV

And what is this matchy that seems all the rage?
I've seen giant catalogues with page after page
Lilac and olive and blush and champagne
We had little choice and we didn't complain

Sparkly jewels on the tack, is this real?
It's frankly appalling, I can't help but feel
Well, when I was young things were simple, just right
Our browbands were plain and our numbnuts were white

CHAPTER 8

What is matchy matchy?

WHAT IS MATCHY MATCHY?

Understanding *matchy matchy* is as critical to success in nag sports as learning whether to turn left or right at *K* or being able to to coax a horse to jump over a comedy model windmill. It's the high fashion of the equine world; it's making sure you and your nag look their best; it's going to a party in this year's latest must-have designs... and you wouldn't want the other horse people to laugh at you, would you? No, you would not.

You see, as explained elsewhere in this book, horse people not only get to spend loads of money dressing themselves up to do riding stuff, they also spend loads of money on clothes for the horse.

And *matchy matchy* is the rule that says that when dressing your horse up like a doll, you're supposed to ensure the various garments are the same colour. It's vital that shit matches.

Now, on the face of it, I get it. Honestly, I do. Stuff looks nice when colours are co-ordinated. I may only be a man, but this isn't rocket surgery. It's not beyond me. My grey car has rather fetching red brake calipers for example and I like that. Though clearly those are two different colours, so maybe I don't get it after all. But I think I do. I get the idea.

But here's where things go pear-shaped for me. You see, I only have the one car and it only has one set of brake calipers. They're red. The car is grey. These are fixed and, within reason, unchangeable. So, the colour thing was a one-time decision. Well, it was second-hand, but the previous owner made a decision I approved of.

But horses, it seems, are like people. They can own many clothes. Many, many clothes.

Now, as previously discussed, horses basically have two main items of clothing — numbnuts and leg warmers — occasionally accessorised with the weird gimp mask. In human terms this is much like a two-piece suit with an optional waistcoat. Stop me if this is going too fast for you.

So initially I thought *matchy matchy* would mean that when the horse needs a new numbnut for example, then it would be very nice if it were to match its leg warmers. Or vice versa. Cool. I get it (see above). It might even be nice to have a second set. Like, I dunno, blue for everyday, casual prancing and red for more formal prancing, when you have the old people making notes at the end of the horse pitch in a Nissan Qashqai.

This seems fair enough to me. It's like my own suits. I actually have three suits currently, in my middle-aged decadence. Until I was about 35, I only ever had one suit. And I don't just mean one at any one time, I mean it was the same suit from 16 onwards. But I finally replaced that in my 30s and eventually added two more.

One's a linen suit for summer weddings, one's tweed

for winter and comedy value, and the third workhorse of a suit is your basic dark blue for weddings in any other season, funerals, job interviews and court appearances. And, a bit like my car's brake calipers, guess how many shirts I match with each? I'll tell you. One. Each suit has one shirt that goes well with it. Clearly I don't have a proper job, but that's another story.

So, I'll allow that it's cool for the horse to have two suits. Why not?

But here's where we get to the crux of this. How many suits does CC2 think the nag should have? About a hundred and fucking fifty from what I can tell. She's made a list and she's ticking them off. Apparently, she already has Visa Violet, Gullible Green, Luscious Lilac and Overdraft Orange. Not just a range of numbnuts, remember, but matching leg warmers too. *Matchy matchy*.

She was given a catalogue by CC1 last year of all the different shit you can buy to dress up horses in all 73,000 colours and asked to mark which she wanted for a Christmas present. She folded the corner of the entire fucking catalogue over and just handed it back, I shit you not. *Matchy matchy? Spendy fucking spendy* more like.

The sad irony of this is that the horse doesn't give two shits how it's been dressed up. As far as I can tell it looks pretty miserable whatever it's wearing, but I think that's just the whole long face thing. It's an old joke but there's some truth in it, right?

The thing that really grips my shit about all of this though, is that much of the matchy stuff isn't even allowed for competitions, at least in prancing. You can have a numbnut, but only in a subdued and boring colour, usually white, but your range of flashy colours aren't going to get a showing. And legwarmers aren't allowed at all, they're just used for casual prancing when nobody's looking. So the matchy isn't just for show, as I might have initially suspected, it's actually much worse than that; it's literally not even *for* show. It's just for looking pretty in while doing practice and lessons.

It's a bit like buying the coolest jacket ever for going to work in, but which contravenes some work dress code, and so you only get to wear it at night. Which would also get a bit hot.

Other disciplines are far less strict than prancing, however, and are a bit more of a free-for-all. They're a lawless bunch, those jumpers and eventers, I tell you, but they seem to be more interested in adrenaline and bobbles than matching shit anyway, so it's all a bit of a waste if you ask me.

Regardless of any actual practical use, or lack of, there are a couple of ways of taking *matchy matchy* even further, once the basics have been mastered.

For example, when employing traditional *matchy matchy*, the general consensus is that everything should be the same colour. The leg warmers, the numbnut and optional gimp mask, don't just co-ordinate with each other but are actually identical. When you think about it, this is a pretty basic take on things.

The next level is *mix 'n' matchy* whereby various colours are used together in a complementary way; this could produce a subtle effect or a shocking one, depending on the colours chosen.

When I was young, I once bought two pairs of Converse boots in different colours so I could wear a red boot on one foot and blue on the other. Or vice versa. I thought I was achingly cool and pushing back the boundaries of fashion. Turns out I was just a twat, but who isn't at 18?

Horses have a distinct advantage in this area though in that they have four legs. So that means you could either have different colours front and back, left and right, or diagonally. Or even all four different, I guess. So many options!

I have to say that I've not actually seen anyone employing *mix 'n' matchy* yet, but I think it's only a matter of time. I suppose you could argue that I've literally just invented it myself, so do credit me if you choose to adopt it.

Another advanced matchy technique is *casual matchy*. This is something that CC2 does quite a lot, and I have to say that it does demand a certain amount of respect, mixed in with the obvious revulsion I initially feel at watching so much of my money just sat on a horse.

The essential idea here is quite straightforward. Matchy shit isn't actually allowed at competitions as already mentioned, so it's really just for use when doing casual prancing. Most people either choose to go full matchy and look as smart as possible, or just lounge about in casual clothes, often hoodies and the like, and to hell with the matchy.

What I've seen CC2 do a fair bit is merge the two together. This means that whenever she's taken to buy new casual clothes, her addled and addicted horse mind dictates that she can only choose things that match her nag matchy shit. So any t-shirt or blouse or jumper actually has to be as closely-matched as possible to Loanshark Lemon or Payday Puce. Nobody will know when she's wearing it with jeans of course; they're just plain coloured tops after all.

What it does mean though, is that when she's having a lesson her entire self is matched perfectly with the nag's clothes, but in a way that tries to say "What, this old thing? Oh, I just found it lying about." It's quite an impressive effect and people walking past tend to stop and whisper to each other, "Do you think that's deliberate? That t-shirt's exactly the same colour as that numbnut!"

I have to applaud CC2's efforts at trying to give the effect of not really trying, while deep down she cares with every ounce of her being to ensure that she matches that fucking nag.

She also does this retrospectively, employing a technique called *reverse matchy*. This is basically deciding that you like an item of already-owned clothing after all because you later discover it matches some of the nag matchy. Allow me to explain.

CC1 bought CC2 three new jumpers a while back. This seems excessive to me, just as a starting point. I last bought a new jumper in 2003, I think. But she's a child and growing, and not just outwards like me, so I'll let her off.

Anyway, CC2 declared these jumpers to be "too square" for her to wear. I'd no idea she was living in 1969 but that's another story. We're obviously just not groovy enough for her. But, suffice it to say, these square, woollen jumpers subsequently lay dormant in some dark and dank corner of CC2's lair for a number of weeks or months (I daren't ask), presumably while CC1 looked everywhere in vain for the missing receipt.

Fast forward to the present day and CC2 re-discovered them and found that, by chance, all three now matched perfectly with some nag matchy that she has. Frankly, the fact that three random colours perfectly match three items from her matchy range tells me one thing and one thing only. She clearly has TOO MANY FUCKING NUMBNUTS. I mean, seriously, what are the chances? How many do you have to own before three random jumpers happen to match three numbnuts perfectly? I don't actually know how many sets she now has of course. I ask CC1 from time to time and get vague answers. Like "Oh, well a few. She has the caramel, and the mustard... and the um... oh, the microwave's just pinged!" as she leaps up and starts talking animatedly about carrots, and then the weather.

These three jumpers have of course now been upgraded in CC2's mind. They are no longer square and shit, they're absolutely essential and wonderful. They now match her matchy. They match the horse. And if something matches the horse then that's just lovely in her world. And so, this is *reverse matchy*. Matching something you already own with the matchy shit you also own.

In many ways I suppose this is a good thing. The jumpers were already bought at least, and were presumably needed. The fact that she now has more matchy, sort of for free is OK, and the fact that she's wearing perfectly good jumpers that we've bought is definitely good. However, I think she's only ever going to wear them while doing prancing practice, so maybe it is wasted money after all.

And for what it's worth, she looks very nice in the jumpers. Even if they are square. I'm not sure what the horse thinks, mind you, but I don't suppose it gives a shit. As usual.

Roses are red
Violets are blue
My numbnut is mustard
My legwarmers too

CHAPTER 9

How do you transport your horse around?

HOW DO YOU TRANSPORT YOUR HORSE AROUND?

At the beginning of your horsing life, if you want to go and do nag stuff it's simply a matter of transporting yourself to your nearest horse hotel and paying the owner to borrow one. Or, as a child, being transported by someone else and having someone else pay someone else to borrow one. The standard M.O. for a child.

This can suffice for a fair while as your nascent addiction starts to form and grow. You could spend years in fact, having weekly lessons and generally fulfilling the needs of a low-level addiction without ever having to engage in the burdensome task of actually moving a tonne of sportscow from one location to another.

But eventually, that day may come when you start entering competitions and needing to move the nag from the luxury of the hotel to some far-flung field of mud in the middle of nowhere to participate in five minutes of prancing or jumping over things. And at this point you're going to look at your beloved nag, scratch your head and think to yourself "How the fuck am I going to shift that lump all the way there?"

You most likely already own a car; let's make that assumption to start with. It's possibly even a big one. I've been to (too) many horse hotels and competitions now and almost everyone has a pretty large car, frequently a big 4x4 of some kind with a massive boot. You might also have a very small pony and start to put two and two together, but it's worth stating from the outset that I don't think this plan has legs, unlike the horse. Which is part of the problem.

Frankly, even if you have a pony small enough to squeeze into the back of your car, you've probably got the same problem that we have — that your car is permanently filled with endless horse-related shit already. I like to refer to our car as the mobile tack room. If, god forbid, I actually need to use the car myself, I have to check the boot first and then empty out a saddle, a chair for the saddle (WTF?), a collection of numbnuts, a horse stick or two and a pile of others things that I can't name because I don't know what they are. But they're all covered in either horse shit, hay, or both, so they're definitely horse-related.

So I'm afraid that, even ignoring the legal dubiousness of squeezing a horse into the back of a car, it's just not going to work. No, I'm afraid that dedicated naguine transport is the only solution to this problem, so you're going to have to start dealing with some pretty stark realisations regarding your impending financial haemorrhage.

The simplest way to approach this problem is to hire something for when it's needed — probably a small trailer. As long as you have a car that's big and powerful enough and has a towbar, then you're golden. You might well have a nice big, powerful 4x4 with a towbar already, in which case there's nothing to see here, please move on. But if you haven't... well, you'll need to buy a new car. A bigger, more expensive one. With a towbar.

Yes, that's right. You need a new car. Sorry about that. This is clearly a recurrent theme when you enter the horsey world; not only do you have to buy a shitload of new, expensive stuff, but you also have to sell some of the really expensive stuff you already own and replace it with more expensive stuff still. This is just how it's going to be, and the sooner you come to terms with that, the easier it's going to be for everyone.

Assuming you now have the right car, and only need the trailer on occasion, then you're probably OK for the time being. It's still not cheap of course; hiring a trailer for the day or weekend isn't exactly peanuts, but it's the cheapest option you have, I'm afraid.

As soon as nag transporting becomes more regular though, you start to question the wisdom of throwing money away each weekend on rent when you could just buy a trailer outright and be done with it. And so you put one foot onto the slippery slope of spending once again, and I'm afraid it's a very long way down this time and there are spikes of debt at the bottom.

Once you've committed to actually buying some form of transport yourself, you can break down the options into four levels of nag taxi:

LEVEL 1

At the bottom end, Level 1 is the humble trailer, as already mentioned. These are merely *expensive* to buy, though if you have to add the cost of a new car then it's a whole other category — but we're keeping it simple for now. And you can tell this is the most utilitarian option as they're usually named in a very prosaic way and called things such as 'NT174e', like a model of washing machine.

You'll need to learn to tow properly with one of these things too, and reversing into a small space is no mean feat until you've had a lot of practice. If we're to believe slapstick comedy, there's also the possibility that the trailer will unhitch itself while you're driving along, and then you'll take one option at a fork in the road and the nag in the trailer will take the other, to hilarious consequence. But assuming you do everything by the book then this is a situation that should be avoidable.

They're also the smallest option to store somewhere when not being used and can often be left at horse hotels by arrangement with the owner, which is good because it means you can avoid the embarrassment of letting your neighbours know that you're a nag addict. You can just sneak out of your neighbourhood in your car like a normal person, and only hitch up the horse and trailer when well out of sight of anyone you might know.

They're also quite practical when at an event itself, as you can unhitch the trailer, leave the nag in it with plenty of hay and then fuck off down the pub in the car.

I bought CC1 a trailer a couple of years ago when I got tired of shelling out cash most weekends over the summer to rent one. In all honesty, it was the very cheapest one I could find, but you could get a horse in it and attach it to a car, so job done in my book. Those qualities are not only the bare essentials of a horse trailer, but pretty much the be all and end all, as far as I'm concerned. The rest is just paint and snobbery.

Luckily, I didn't have to see it very often as it was kept at the horse hotel the nag was booked into. So it was about a year after she'd sold it that I even noticed we didn't have one any more. I'd tell you why it got sold if I only I could remember what she told me at the time, but the upshot is that she decided it wasn't up to scratch in some way, sold it and I never saw the money again. Presumably it got converted into *matchy matchy* shit, and so lives on as a set of caramel legwarmers and matching iPhone case.

I think perhaps that my plan of buying the cheapest one I could find may have backfired. It was possibly just a little *too* shit, and there were inevitable costs looming just to keep it legal and usable. A warning there perhaps.

LEVEL 2

Level 2 is the 3.5 tonne horsebox. Something converted from a modest van. These are *very expensive* and are named similarly to caravans, so are called things like 'Concorde Deluxe' and 'Idris Elba XL'. These are big enough for a nag or two but not so big that you need any special skills or licences to drive, and so are seen as the ideal upgrade from a Level 1. There are some downsides though. Primarily, there seems to be some weird rule that this level of vehicle needs to be painted in a vile colour scheme (claret and purple, mmmm!) and then have a child's sketch of a prancing horse down the sides. I assume this is a ploy by the manufacturers to encourage you to buy a Level 3 instead. It also means that you can't park it on a driveway and pretend it's just a normal van, so if you're in the market for a Level 2, then try and hold out for a plain one.

The other main downside is that although they're

pretty big compared to a car, they're not really that big once you've squeezed a horse and all the *matchy matchy* shit into the back of them. Most of the time they don't come with any extra space for the humans to sleep in — the 'living'. At best they sometimes have a small area to keep out of the rain during the day. And in my experience, rain is inevitable at these events. It seems to follow horses around like the flies do.

This is the reason CC1 doesn't want a Level 2. Apparently, for any future transport purchase I make it's vital that it 'has living' so that CC1 and CC2 can stay the night at various distant horse pitches around the country, and so prance far and wide with wild abandon.

The thing is, you don't actually have to buy a massive lorry just to spend a night away from home, surely? I myself used to travel the country to enjoy a sport (when I still had my own money) and I found the perfect vehicle that 'had living': it was my car. And a fucking tent. 39 quid, job done.

So, if you're the pampered kind that requires soft cotton sheets at night and the luxury of toilet facilities, then you're either going to have to keep splashing out for a hotel or raise your sights upwards to the giddy heights of the next level.

LEVEL 3

And now we're getting exotic. It's the full-on 7.5 tonne option. The big, fuck-off nag taxi that'll store as many sportscows as you're ever likely to need and still have room left over for a kitchen designed for dwarves and some beds secreted somewhere up a little ladder. You do sometimes get a toilet and a shower though, but the downside is that they're often the same thing.

The benefits of a Level 3 are really just size and space. Not only can you sleep in them, but you can store a whole load more shit in them. Shit for the horse in the front, actual horse shit in the back. If we ever owned one of these then it'd basically just be a way of storing the endless numbnuts and legwarmers we seem to have. It'd be like a giant horse wardrobe on wheels — though at least we'd free up half of our house and I'd be able to get to the frozen sausages again.

There seem to be two sub-classes of this level: new ones that are *really really expensive*, and others that were built in 1963 and have 'only done 4.3 million miles'. Sometimes these still have the prancing horse sketch, but less often it seems. They do have to have 'Caution Horses' on the back though I think, and this has always annoyed me. Where's the comma? Eh? Or better still, a semi-colon. What the fuck is a Caution Horse? It sounds like it's some mystical wise being, dispensing circumspect financial advice. "Oh, so you think I should avoid a lease on a new car until I've paid off my mortgage? Hmm, good advice, Caution Horse, thanks!"

LEVEL 4

This is the 'over 7.5 tonne' category and priced at the *fuck me!* level of expense. Though it's hard to be specific because they're usually just marked up as 'POA', which I think stands for 'Piss Off, Amateur'. You know you're at the classy end of the market now because they're not pink or purple any more, but soothing shades of expensive-looking greys. They're also now called regal things like

'The Buckingham' or 'The Sandringham' that are supposed to ooze class. The good ones have satellite dishes on the top. The really good ones have their own satellites.

I have to confess to enjoying the ads for these though, because they're quite splendid. They tend to feature attractive young people wearing suspiciously-clean white horse clothes, having champagne receptions in 'the living' while chortling at some unseen joke, before reclining back in a miniaturised four-poster to watch TV on a 42". I hope the walls are thick enough between the luxury living on one side and all that horse piss that's pooled up on the other side.

When you start seriously looking at classified ads for these varying levels of transport, you'll start to learn the kind of words that are a bad sign and ones which are better. I've learnt to be fearful of words such as 'luxury', 'bespoke', 'tailored', 'premium', 'style', 'stunning' or 'deluxe', but do like the words 'affordable' and 'legal'.

It goes without saying that CC1 thinks of herself more of a Sandringham customer than a NT174e kind, but she seems to have settled in her mind on the 7.5 tonne Level 3 as her next transport, as if this is some kind of compromise I've won. She's actually said before that if it was me that was into horses then I'd have bought a beautiful and splendid lorry by now. This of course is quite hurtful and very unfair! Completely true of course, but that's hardly the point.

Frankly I'm not a fan of spending that much money at all on anything nag-related, and I don't have any money left even if I was. CC1 however has worked it all out and decided that a Level 3 would be cheaper in the long run, once we've taken into account the money saved on trailer rental and staying at hotels, but I'm not buying it. The argument, I mean. But the horsebox too.

I get accused of employing Man Maths all the time by CC1. Like when I say I should buy a new motorbike because it would be more economical than my older one. It'd just cost an extra four grand. And I'd save £63 every year in fuel!

But I feel that CC1 has taken this to extremes with her lorry logic. I think the world should recognise the evils of Horse Maths. This is way more powerful and fucked up than mere Man Maths. I've never once tried to justify buying a whole fucking lorry. That drone I've got my eye on seems completely trivial by comparison.

So, I'm going to try and employ the last option, which I also present to you as an alternative if you're keen to minimise expenditure. Sadly though, it only really works when you're financing a child rather than buying for yourself. And that's simply to try and hold out for so long that she'll have grown up, taken her driving test, got a job and saved up enough to buy her own damned taxi before I have to.

I'm not confident this will work though, as I'll have to wait at least another 10 years, but I'll stay strong for as long as I can. For those of you who can't choose this option, I'm afraid you're going to have to resign yourself to spending a few hours poring over the classifieds with a calculator to hand. It's not going to be pretty.

Good luck.

Some are massive
Some are small
Some are like the Albert Hall

Some are speedy
Most are slow
Some require a car to tow

Some are painted
With great pride
With a horse sketch down the side

Some are rusty
Some are new
Some were made in '62

Some have warnings
Shown to all
'Caution Horses' three foot tall

Some take one horse
For a ride
Some take two nags side by side

Some cost little
Most do not
It all depends how much you've got

CHAPTER 10

What horse sports can you compete in?

WHAT HORSE SPORTS CAN YOU COMPETE IN?

Once you've perfected the art of getting onto the horse and not falling off, have obtained all the saddles and rigging the nag needs and dressed it up in a load of *matchy matchy* shit it doesn't need, the next question you have to ask yourself is this: well, now what?

For some, there may not need to be any more. You can go to the hotel each day and do all the stroking, feeding and shit-picking you want to and then maybe go out for a little stroll together. Just wander out into the wild occasionally and get into adventures. But for others, the world of competitive horse sports is now calling, because your horse life up to this point clearly hasn't been expensive or dangerous enough.

So, what are the options? Well, there are quite a few different sports out there and it really depends on what you want to get out of it that will lead you to a well-suited choice. If you're seeking an adrenaline rush and want to experience thrills, high speeds and danger then you'll probably want to discount dressage for example.

If, on the other hand, you want to haemorrhage cash as quickly as possible for tax reasons, then you need look no further than polo. And if you're simply looking for a way to pursue a profitable career that'll handsomely reward your interest in horses then I suggest you give up entirely, sell the nag and just become a vet.

The exciting news is that once you've settled on a discipline to pursue, you now get to go out and secure a brand-new loan to spend on a whole load of new shit. You might need a new range of clothes for both you and the horse, possibly a new saddle even. And if your current pony is a gentle little plodder but you've now set your heart on showjumping then it's quite possibly going to be goodbye to Mr Bubbles and hello to Fireflash, or whatever ridiculous names they have.

Unless of course you decide to move into polo, and then it'll be hello to Fireflash, Fireflash 2, Pinky, Winky, Wonky, Dinky, Big Johnny, Scampi, Sailor, Dave Dee, Dozy, Beaky, Mick, Tich and the rest of the gang you'll need to buy.

DRESSAGE

Dressage, or to give it its proper name, prancing, is where you and your trot donkey go onto a horse pitch and walk around a bit together. Sometimes you have to go in a straight line and sometimes not. It's incredibly dull. The pitches come in two different sizes and can be either indoors or outdoors. I mention these details not because they're particularly important but because it's about the most interesting thing there is to say about it.

There are no jumps, no obstacles, not even a clock to ride against. It's literally just gentle prancing around while you go 'tra la la la' in your head and think about what to have for dinner that evening.

Of course, it's not actually that simple. Well, it sort of is but I'm going to play devil's advocate for a bit to pad this out. It's about the rider's mastery of the horse and their ability to memorise and follow a set of pre-defined moves as accurately as possible. With horse and ride in perfect harmony, they are able to carry out the test with pinpoint accuracy, displaying grace and economy of input. So, basically it's walking around a bit, as I said.

Letters are placed around the pitch and these are used as markers to aim for as the test progresses. To up the excitement levels, these are placed in a non-alphabetical order. Woah! You're interested now, aren't you?! Never let it be said that dressage people don't live life on the edge. Nobody actually knows why they're in the order they are, fascinatingly enough, but it's always the same and so the first thing a budding prancer needs to do is learn the letters.

On a small pitch the order is A, K, E, H, C, M, B, F. The way to remember these is to commit a mnemonic to memory: Any Kids Enjoying Horses Cost Massively Big Funds. On the big pitch the letters are A, K, V, E, S, H, C, M, R, B, P, F, and the mnemonic for this is: Any Kids Venturing into Equine Sports? Heed Caution, Means Robbing the Bloody Pension Fund.

It's useful to learn these letters even if you're just funding a child and not participating yourself, as a constant reminder of the financial world of pain you're entering. It's also vitally important that you ensure any child prancers are made to learn these same mnemonics so that you can instill a sense of guilt into them as early as possible. This is bound to come in useful later on.

From here you need to get some training with a specialist, because you don't want to risk exposing yourself to the dangers of competition without being fully prepared. The dangers in this case are mainly to do with going the wrong way and looking a bit of a tit rather than risking life and limb, but sometimes that's actually worse, so get yourself skilled up.

Trainers are a funny breed and seem to share a series of odd traits amongst them. The way it works is that they usually stand in the middle of a practice pitch and watch as the trainee and nag walk in circles around them. What's odd is that they always hold their heads at a 45-degree angle, as if they can only assess a horse and rider whilst imagining they're walking up a particularly steep hill.

The other rule they seem to have is that they're always holding a mug of tea or coffee while they do the training. I initially wondered whether this was just used as a hand warmer in the colder months, but I think it's mainly used as a prop to make them look more important. "You're out on the horse, working hard and doing what I tell you, but check me out, I'm just having a quick coffee!" They do have to be careful though as trying to drink while still having their heads lolling at 45 degrees is a recipe for disaster.

Sunglasses are another useful prop. Again, they ensure the trainer looks cool, but also they can hide any unwanted expression that might show through in the trainer's eyes: disappointment, derision, boredom. It wouldn't surprise me at all if they actually have their eyes closed for some of the time while they daydream about being on a beach somewhere rather than standing on some cut-up car tyres in the freezing cold holding a mug of coffee for warmth.

The best thing though is the shouting. A lot of them

shout non-stop commands at the prancing trainee and I like that bit. I like watching someone else shout at my child. I don't know if that's wrong of me or not, but it's like watching someone else do a household chore for me. In my experience as a piss-poor parent, it seems that children need shouting at for much of the day, so I'm like "You take over the shouting at the child for a bit, I'll be sat over there with a cup of tea. I'll take over again in an hour."

Also, I sort of weirdly enjoy listening to them bark instructions because it's all complete and utter nonsense to my ears, and so there's a kind of weird melodic pleasure to be had by it. It'd be boring if I understood anything, but luckily I don't, so I listen with amusement to trainers shouting at CC2. "Loosen your hat stand! What are you doing with your big toe?! Bring him back under, he's trying to play Monopoly with you! Tighten your underscrew, it's going sideways! HANDS!!"

It seems to be a lot to do with tightening and loosening various things, and it's always the fault of the hands. This much I've learnt. But it has a hypnotic quality to it, specifically because I have no fucking idea what they're on about. It's like listening to the shipping forecast on the radio, which is similarly poetical nonsense to me. "Dogging, rising level in the east, 14, lowering to orange around noon." Love it.

I often look to CC2 who'll be nodding understanding at each barked command to loosen or tighten something and sometimes wonder if they're in it together just to take the piss out of me. Like they got together beforehand to plot the whole thing. "Right, I'll shout complete bollocks at you and then you nod and pretend it's real. Then just watch his stupid face, all furrowed in confusion with his eyes swivelling back and forth between us. It'll be hilarious! And he's paying a fortune for it!"

Bastards. I'm getting genuinely quite angry thinking about this now, and I just made it up. I think.

I do actually make an effort to go and watch CC2 being trained a fair bit. Apart from enjoying watching her being shouted at, I also like watching where my money's going. I don't like watching it actually go of course, but if it's going to go then I like to be there in person to supervise it and make sure nothing bad happens to the rest of it.

Once you or your progeny have been fully trained in the art of prancing, the next thing to do is actually enter a competition and prove your worth. These are dreadful affairs. Basically, a load of people drive to some pre-arranged location with a horse pitch, usually in the absolute middle of nowhere, and ideally in about a foot of cold, wet mud.

I had to spend two days and a night at one last summer with CC1 and CC2 and it was miserable. It rained of course, incessantly, and there was nothing to do at all apart from sit in a damp tent and listen to horses freaking out over gentle breezes and wellies. It was like Glastonbury but without the bands or the drugs. Or the food stalls. Or the fun.

It was so wet that CC1 actually gave up on our tent and went to sleep in the boot of the car. I instead opted for the tried-and-tested camping technique I've employed on many occasions over the years, which requires one tent, a sleeping bag and two bottles of wine. You simply drink all the wine and then spend 20 minutes trying to wriggle into the sleeping bag until you pass out exhausted, ideally until morning. When you regain consciousness, you can score yourself on the percentage of your body that actually made it into the bag. I got 68% so I actually beat CC2 that weekend, on points.

Most of her events are smaller affairs though, and don't require staying overnight. I find I can usually drive over, get as wet, muddy and miserable as I need to within the hour and be back home in time for Top Gear. It's not like it makes much difference if I actually get to watch her or not anyway. To be honest, I find I can rarely work out which one she is once she's in her gear. Small girl, yay high, white horse trousers and blue jacket, sat on a brown horse. She hardly stands out. And once you've seen one 20m circle, you've seen them all. I once spent 10 minutes providing steadfast and fatherly moral support, concentrating hard on CC2's performance, willing her with all my mental energy to turn right at 'H' or whatever the fuck she was supposed to be doing, when I got a text from CC1. Turned out they were at a service station half way home and were just checking to see if I wanted anything.

It's not like you can even offer much in the way of support anyway. There's no cheering or clapping to be done. You have to stand there, stock still, hands in pockets, doing an impression of a shit ventriloquist if you need to whisper anything. Horses are as neurotic as an old lady that's run out of valium and just walk around the horse pitch, brow furrowed and eyes swivelling suspiciously from side to side, trying to catch sight of anything they can have a bloody good spook at so they can Go Fucking Mental for a laugh. Every time I see one enter the ring with some poor little girl clinging on tight, the theme tune to Casualty pops into my head. I once saw someone turn left instead of right at 'K' and raised an eyebrow in mild surprise. That was enough to send the trot donkey into panic and it reared up, flung off its rider and sprinted out of the venue, gleefully enjoying its little moment.

That last bit didn't happen of course, I made it up. There's no way in hell I'd know whether they were supposed to turn left or right at 'K'. I'm usually staring at the ceiling by then anyway, trying to count all the hanging light fixtures and being amazed by how much dust they can carry and how it all got so high up.

The whole affair is scored by a pair of old ladies who watch intently and then pass judgement. They sit in little judging sheds at the end of the horse pitch, with a Thermos flask of tea and some sandwiches. If there's no shed, then they just drive up in their Nissan Qashqais and park there. This is actually preferable for them because if they get bored they can just put some music on, or listen to Radio 4.

You'd expect the scores to be something like 'pretty good' or 'reasonable' or something fairly vague like that. It's pretty hard to score someone walking around a bit and sometimes going in a circle. But the scores are actually percentages and come out as figures like 63.4785%. The kind of complicated numbers that you might get as an answer in a maths exam, usually as a sign that you've probably made a mistake somewhere.

I'm not suggesting they just make them up, but I do wonder if they add on a digit or two at the end just to make it look more scientific. It's especially hard to mark the freestyle, which is when the rider makes it up as they go along while they play shit music over the tannoy. All very odd.

At the end of the event, the top riders get a rosette, which is basically a flimsy piece of cotton and paper. CC2 loves winning rosettes and considers them a true badge of honour. I, on the other hand, consider them a pretty fucking disappointing reward for all the money it cost to pay for the competition entry, the trailer hire, a tank of petrol and some shit sandwiches, but then she's got around 30 years to work on her bitterness still.

Like many other nag addicts, she proudly displays hers on her bedroom wall at home. To her they're priceless, though I've calculated that each one has cost me around £764, so she'd damned well better look after them. I often think this whole charade could be greatly simplified if I just bought a whole box of them for a tenner, left them in her room and sold the horse.

SHOWJUMPING AND EVENTING

Showjumping is pretty straightforward when compared to prancing. Jumps are set up around the pitch and then the nag and rider have to navigate around the course and, well, jump over them. Clue's in the name really. The jumps get higher and higher as you progress up the ranks, though they're set up in such a way that they fall over pretty much just by looking at them funny, so there's no real danger of the nag hurting itself on them.

The horse, alas, doesn't know this, so there's still every chance that it'll decide against jumping it after all, and hence there's a bit more drama than there usually is with the prancing.

Eventing is like the 'Best of' compilation album of horse sports, though admittedly there are only three songs on it. Riders have to do prancing and showjumping and a thing called crosscountry, either all in one day or over three days. The prancing and jumping sections are as previously described, but when you watch the cross country bit you realise that eventers are basically mentally ill.

Unlike in showjumping, event jumps do not fall over in a light breeze but are completely solid. Hit a showjumping pole and it falls over; hit an eventing jump and *you* fall over. Some are just lazy piles of railway sleepers or logs, but sometimes they're more cutesy and made to look like miniature houses or covered wagons or some shit. It's like a cross between a battle scene from Braveheart and crazy golf.

If you've come from a prancing background, then it looks like really angry dressage but on fast forward. Like when you're sat on the TV remote by mistake. And the riders talk to their horses like they're people. I get yer basic encouragements... 'Good boy!', 'Wooah there', that kind of thing. The gentle, patronising sorts of things you say to any animal, but these people actually engage in conversation with their nags the whole way round the pitch. They're galloping round at a million miles an hour, chatting away. "No Blackie, not that way, we talked about this. Left, Blackie, left, remember?! No Blackie, number 12 next, can't you count?" No, they can't count, you fucking lunatic. You need sectioning.

It's definitely more exciting than prancing though. I don't mean to downplay dressage of course, which as we all know is all about control, attention to detail, the beautiful synergy between man and horse, blah, blah, blah, but they need to start adding jumps to bring the crowds in. If you feel the need to be thrown off your horse before being dragged by your ankles through a comedy windmill while being lovingly trampled, then eventing is definitely the horse sport for you.

It's worth pointing out though that their *matchy matchy* is pretty shit. They try, bless them, but don't seem to have the attention to detail that the prancers display. Like, they might go for a bright blue numbnut and matching ear warmers, and then let it all go with an entirely different shade of blue for their own shirt! Pathetic! They do make up for it though with comedy bobbles on their woolly hats. I've asked several people why they wear these and nobody seems to know. It's like a badge of honour I think that says, "I'm really tough and do eventing", except the badge itself is a small tuft of soft wool, so it does seem a bit misplaced.

POLO

Polo is another horse sport, as well as a mint. This is where things really start to get out of control. With prancing and showjumping for example, you need a reasonable-sized pitch. Cross country requires a bit of countryside and some logs. But polo requires a field the size of Belgium because they're going flat out most of the time and cover a significant amount of ground.

But the actual pitch is the least of polo's decadence. The main problem with getting into polo is that you'll need to buy a few thousand new horses, as each player gets through hundreds each match. It's got so bad that some top players now genetically engineer new nags as it simply takes too long to wait for new ones to be born.

Buying (or growing) these endless 'strings' of ponies, transporting them around the world for matches and hiring Belgium-sized pitches is naturally fantastically expensive. Luckily, almost all polo players are incredibly rich, at least to start with, so that problem can be worked around. If you're not hugely rich yourself then you might want to think about avoiding it as a sport and concentrating on one of the merely *expensive* horse sports instead.

You can however go and watch polo as a spectator. This is actually very enjoyable even if you're not much of a horse person. This is because nobody actually watches the game itself but simply gets drunk nearby on expensive champagne and Pimms while showing off their expensive picnic hampers and new hats. The polo is what happens as a sort of backdrop to the main event, as if you were attending a royal tea party with a small, Napoleonic battle going on behind you. You could turn around to watch if you wanted, but it would seem a bit rude to the person talking to you.

Like American Football, the game goes on almost indefinitely but with endless breaks. At these points, spectators are encouraged to drain their glasses, have one last strawberry and then stagger drunkenly onto the pitch to help replace the divots and therefore repair the pitch for the next session.

This is a complete waste of time because everyone is so drunk by this point, especially in the latter hours of the game, that trying to repair the damage done by hundreds of wild horses wheeling around a huge swathe of land with a few wobbly stilettos is an exercise in futility. All you can see for miles around is people stumbling around the pitch clutching half-empty bottles of Bollinger while all the alpha males shout "Come on! Divots everybody!"

Eventually, the spectators get cleared off the pitch and everyone goes back to their picnic blankets and resumes their conversations about whether to buy the new Range Rover or not.

After about 10 hours of playing, Argentina is declared the winner and everyone packs up and goes home.

There is a variant of this game called water polo. This should only be attempted if your horse is a good swimmer.

OTHER SPORTS

There are of course a large number of other horse sports available around the world, though it's unlikely the casual horse person is going to have much opportunity to enjoy them.

Perhaps the most popular is horse racing, which itself has endless variations. But unless you're a tiny little man, probably from Ireland, then it's unlikely you'll make much headway here.

In the States there's the rodeo and this covers a wide range of nag-related events. I'm not even going to pretend I've actually been to a rodeo so I'm not going to be able to give much detail here, but I've read about it and it all sounds pretty fucked up. You just have to see the names of the events to get the general gist: pole bending, goat tying, steer wrestling. The latter is the one where the rider jumps off his horse onto the back of a massive cow which he then attempts to wrestle to the ground by grabbing its horns.

Now, I'm not going to try and pigeon-hole the readers of this book, and I'm certainly not going to try and tell you how to live your lives, but I suggest that if you're an accountant from Dorking who enjoys hacking your pony on the odd weekend and perusing the glittery horse tiaras in the catalogues in your spare time, then perhaps steer wrestling isn't for you. I'm not telling you, I'm just saying.

Goat tying is more genteel, and merely involves leaping off your horse, grabbing a goat, throwing it to the ground and tying it up. Naturally, this is aimed more at the women and children.

Further afield, the number and range of horse sports becomes ever wider. In Mongolia, horses outnumber people over 7 to 1, a statistic I'm sure CC2 would approve of heartily. Here, nags have been a central part of their culture for hundreds of years, and jockeys in races can be as young as five.

And in the central Asian region covering Afghanistan, Kyrgyzstan, Tajikistan, Kazakhstan and other countries with excellent Scrabble-scoring names, the ancient sport of Buzkashi is very popular. Here, one team of mounted horse people attempt to transport the headless carcass of a goat from one point of the pitch to another to score a goal, while the opposing team try to capture it, possibly by whipping or attempting to otherwise knock the other riders off their horses, depending on the regional rules.

This is also a children's sport. No, not really. But it does sound like a pretty entertaining spectator sport.

So, if you're looking at the range of sports available to you and are trying to decide whether eventing is too dangerous compared to prancing, then do keep in mind that neither involves a headless goat or jumping onto a live (and possibly angry) cow. Also, my personal favourite, jousting, appears to have faded in popularity in the last few hundred years, so you won't have to worry about being smashed in the chest while riding at speed, or buying a whole new *matchy matchy* suit of armour. Or joust storage, and that's a detail not to be overlooked when you think about it.

Full of fright
Head feels light
Make sure the girth is done up tight

In we go
For the show
Horse is being a so-and-so

Centre line
Feeling fine
Might actually do ok this time

What's my score
They're on the door
Well bugger me, it's 64!

THAT'S ALL, FOLKS

Well, sadly that concludes the main part of this tome.

If, by reading this book, you're now feeling all fired up and keen to get more involved, perhaps even wanting to source your first nag and launch into a lifetime of competitive equine sports, then good for you! Hopefully you'll now be armed with some valuable information that will help guide your choices along the way.

If, on the other hand, you've somehow been a bit put off horses and horse sports then I'm sorry. A bit.

Don't be mad at me though. You'll probably come to realise at some point down the line that I've done you a favour. I'll have certainly saved you some cash however you look at it. I accept both cheques and wine in lieu of any gift you'd like to forward onto to me in thanks.

In conclusion I'd like to summarise what I've learnt about our equine chums over the last few years. Clearly, I've learnt a lot looking at the density of wisdom packed into this book, but I feel this can all be distilled into 8 key points, as below.

1. Although they look similar, there are actually several different types of horse sport.

2. Although nominally different, there are actually only three different colours of horse.

3. Horses, like people, wear both clothes and shoes. Some are functional (e.g. numbnuts) and some just for fashion (e.g. legwarmers).

4. Making all the clothes match each other, and optionally match the horse person on top, is apparently of vital importance.

5. Horses are generally very pampered and get to stay in the best hotels and have their own personal taxis to drive them around in.

6. Horses are paranoid as fuck and therefore inherently pretty dangerous to be near.

7. Horses can be highly addictive and so any contact with them should be thought about long and hard beforehand.

8. Everything related to horses is expensive.

I think that's it. That basically sums up everything I know about horses. Good luck with your own journey!

GLOSSARY

Water polo

GLOSSARY

Bay
A brown horse.

Bit
The thing between the teeth. Also, the exact opposite of how much it'll all cost.

Beans
You don't want to know. Trust me, you really don't want to know. I found out by accident and instantly regretted knowing. If you really need to know then ask someone else. I'm not talking about it.

Blood chestnut
A brown horse.

Box rest
When you're tired from having to watch horse sports and need to relax with a box of wine you snuck in with you.

Buckskin
A brown horse.

Casual matchy
The art of accidentally-on-purpose matching your casual attire to your nag's when merely having a lesson or other casual occasion. *SEE Matchy matchy*

Casual prancing
Practising prancing for fun or as part of a lesson. Distinct from *formal prancing*.

Cavaletti
A pasta dish.

CC1
Cost Centre One. My other half, mother of our child and general financial burden to me.

CC2
Cost Centre Two. Our horse-mad, eleven-year-old daughter, whose addiction to nags, dressage and *matchy matchy* is the ruin of me.

Charlotte Dujardin
Charlotte of the garden is CC2's hero. She saw her once at Olympia and practically assaulted her in trying to get a photo taken with her.

Chestnut
A brown horse.

Dun
A brown horse.

Fly rug
The tiniest rug in the world, suitable for keeping flies warm. No idea what is has to do with horses.

Fly sheet
The small specks of insect droppings found in Spain.

Forelock
The thing I tug when demanded to buy something connected with the nag.

Formal prancing
Doing prancing in front of an actual old lady judge at a competition. *SEE Casual prancing*

Freestyle
The form of dressage where you get to make it up as you go along.

Fresian
A type of cow.

Frog
A squashed amphibian under the horse's hoof.

Full shitpicking
The full-board option at a horse hotel where the shit is all picked up for you 7 days a week. Choose this one. *SEE Part shitpicking, PIY, Horse hotel*

Gee-gee junkie

A person hopelessly addicted to nags, horse sports and everything related.

Gelding

A horse without its pony nuts.

Gimp mask

A special mask for making your horse look like a badass. The horse can then indulge in roadside banditry, sexual deviation or Mexican wrestling.

Girth

The circumference of a horse's penis.

Glue

Your beloved nag, eventually.

GFM (Going Fucking Mental)

The thing a horse starts doing when it gets spooked. *SEE Spooking*

Hacking

Riding a horse where you're almost certainly not supposed to, and probably ending up with getting lost somewhere, in the rain. Also, the type of cough you get after getting lost somewhere, in the rain.

Holiday

The thing you used to have every summer before you, or a member of your family, decided to get a horse. Ironically, it's also the thing you now need more than ever.

Horse hotel
The luxury accommodation that horses hang out in.

Horse maths
The evil form of mathematics that allows someone to calculate that spending a fortune on a horsebox will somehow work out cheaper than just renting a trailer and staying in a hotel.

Horse stick
A special stick for dropping whilst sat on a horse, so you can order other people around to pick it up for you.

Horse stroking
The act of brushing, washing or merely caressing your nag. Has to be done at least daily, especially after being ridden.

Horse tax
The tax applied to any item sold in connection to horses that turns the most modest item into one that's bizarrely expensive.

Horse tiara
The strip of rigging that goes across the nag's forehead and used to display all the shiny tat you can fit on.

Judging shed
The shed used by formal event judges to sit in while they make notes, eat sandwiches and drink tea. Can be replaced by a Nissan Qashqai where none is available. *SEE Nissan Qashqai*

Jumper

Sounds cheap but isn't. Not made of wool.

Laminitis

The negative reaction to seeing too many laminated warning signs around a horse hotel.

Leg warmers

80s-style fashion accessory, popular with trendy disco horses.

Liver chestnut

A brown horse.

Marbles

An innocent childhood game played with small glass balls. Also, something horrific and terrifying that you really don't want to know about.

Matchy matchy

Dressing your horse up like it's a doll. *SEE Reverse matchy matchy, Mix 'n' matchy*

Mealy chestnut

A brown horse.

Ménage

Something to do with group sex.

Mix 'n' matchy

Going wild with *matchy matchy* and really pushing the boat out. *SEE Matchy matchy*

Mobile tack room

A car.

Mud

The setting for all horse-related sport. Get used to it.

Mud fever

The reaction to spending all day standing around in mud. The reaction itself takes many forms, but the usual antidote is alcohol. *SEE Wine*

Muzzle

The thing I think about looking down sometimes when I realise what my life has become.

Naghat

A crown that horse people wear, but slightly more expensive.

Naganomics

Naguine financial accounting. *SEE Naguine*

Nagaphernalia

All the shit that comes with a horse and ends up filling the entirety of your car boot and several rooms of your house.

Nagative

Something bad about horses. See pages 1-173 for details.

Nag taxi

The personal transport that your horse gets chauffeured around in.

Naguine
Adjective to describe horse-related stuff.

Nissan Qashqai
Favoured vehicle of event judges. Parked next to the pitch and used as a place to judge from when there's no shed available. SEE *Judging shed*

Numbnut
The thing that goes under the saddle. Used to match colours with the other horse clothes and for showing off the 'sponsorship' you got from your dad's company.

Part shitpicking
The accommodation package at a horse hotel where the shit is all picked up for you Mon-Fri, but you have to come and deal with it on weekends. SEE *Full shitpicking*, *PIY*, *Horse hotel*

Piaffe
A dressage move that involves the horse pretending to be a comedy cartoon burglar sneaking past a window. Named after a French singer.

Pig's trotter
A police horse.

Pitch
Any area within which horse games are played.

PIY (Pick It Yourself)
The cheapest accommodation package at a horse hotel, whereby you get to pick up all the shit yourself. SEE *Part shitpicking, Full shitpicking, Horse hotel*

Polo
A horse sport for very rich people where you speed up and down a large horse pitch making as much of a mess as possible so that you can then stop every so often and make poorer people tidy it up for you. Also, a mint.

Poo-picking
A sweet and cutesy way of describing the picking up barrow-loads of shit from a field.

Reverse matchy matchy
Justifying the purchase of a previously-discarded piece of clothing once you find out it nicely matches some horse clothes. SEE *Matchy matchy*

Rigging
All the bits of leather and rope that are strapped onto and around the horse to hold everything in place and give you something to hold onto.

Rosette
A thoroughly disappointing reward for spending a whole shitload of money.

Saddle *verb*
To cause someone to have a problem or burden, usually debt.

Saddle tree
A mythical tree in a faraway, magical land where saddles grow, for free.

Sandy bay
A brown horse. Also, the name of about a million different shit caravan parks and campsites.

Shoe
A bent iron bar nailed to the foot of a horse, designed to churn up areas of grass.

Spooking
The thing that horses do when they sense something is not right with the world. Like a leaf is out of place, or a fly has taken an unexpected turn to the left. *SEE Going Fucking Mental (GFM)*

String
Sounds cheap, but actually means more horses than you can afford.

Sweet itch
The condition that arises when you're sat around watching a child or partner practicing or competing and you really want a biscuit to go with a cup of tea you have.

Tacky room
Special room at a horse hotel for storing all the gaudy bits of rigging with plastic 'jewels' and sequins stuck all over them.

Valegro

A brown horse and the most famous dressage horse in the world. Not only can it go left or right on command, it can also juggle whilst riding a skateboard. Named after a 1970s brown Austin car.

Wine

The only known antidote to horses.

Water Polo

A team sport for horses that can swim. Also, a soggy mint.

THE END

You got to the end, congratulations!

If you enjoyed this book, please, please do consider leaving a review on Amazon — it makes a huge difference to small, self-published authors like me who rely entirely on word-of-mouth.

When I say 'small', I don't mean in stature necessarily, I just mean in terms of staff (zero) and marketing budget (zero). I'm an entirely normal height, honestly.

If you're a member of Goodreads, then that's also a lovely place to leave a review. Any mentions on social media are obviously immensely appreciated too.

That's it, begging over.

If you didn't enjoy this book then I'm very, very sorry. I'm not sure what we do now, it's all got a bit awkward. You could burn it I suppose, if that'll make you feel any better? I won't mind. Don't do this if you're reading the Kindle version though, that would be a terrible mistake. Alternatively, if you really thought it was awful and that nobody could possibly enjoy it, you could just give it to someone you don't like. They'll only stick it in the downstairs loo anyway, and that would be kind of fitting in this case.

If you'd like to read more of this kind of nonsense on a regular basis, then do follow me on my Facebook page where I post regularly about the day-to-day goings on with CC1, CC2 and the nags.

I also post some stuff on Instagram and Twitter occasionally, though I often forget to. Please follow me wherever you like.

On top of that, you can sign up to my newsletter and receive incredibly sporadic updates about any new books or other big news. I won't spam you, I promise. In fact, I send about one email every couple of years, I should really do more with it. But there you go. You can sign up from my website or from my Facebook page, in theory at least. It might be broken, I'll check.

 @skintdressagedaddy

 @skintdressagedaddy

 @dressagedaddy

 www.skintdressagedaddy.com

If you enjoyed this book but thought it needed a bit more animation, then ***Nag Hotel*** may be just your thing.

Follow the adventures of Prince and Geoffrey, the miserable old codger and his hapless 'friend', as they stagger from one disaster to another.

There are two seasons of episodes and they're only a couple of minutes long each, so you don't waste too much time... though there's also a Christmas Special that's a feature-length 9 minutes!

Contains swearing and references to smoking, drinking, drugs, sex & violence. Suitable for all ages.

(Season 3 *may* be coming in 2022!)

If you'd like to share your own amusing nag-related photos, videos, jokes or anecdotes, then join the **Nagland** group on Facebook.

It's basically just a load of horse people sharing fun and funny horse stuff from themselves and around the internet.

Go to **facebook.com/groups/naglandgroup**